Complete Twerks
Poems, stories, and absurdities

by

Mary Lister

Darkmoor Books

Front cover: Mary Lister, from *Gods Walking Dogs*.
Illustrations by Mary Lister, designed by Polly Walker.
Fair Knights illustration by Polly Walker.
ISBN: 9798872780694
Edited by: Polly R. Walker, Darkmoor Books
Copyright: Mary Lister, 2024, All rights reserved.

Dedication

To Djenna, Freddy, and Arthur, my grandchildren.

Also by the author

Poetry collections:

Trapezing in the Dark

In the Company of Poets – Holme Valley Poets

Books for children:

Winter King and Summer Queen

Princess Polly to the Rescue

Princess Polly and the Magic Megaplot

The Curse of the Macabres

Creepo Macabre and the Beast of Loch Horar

Contents

Foreword 1

Part 1: Linguistical Twerks of Life and Love (In Different Registers) 3

    Geography Lovers 5
    The Tinder Love of the Couch Potatoes 6
    Clichés. A Love Song 7
    Revelations in Soap Operas 9
    Musical Passion 11
    Last Tango in Orpington 12
    A Medieval Nightmare: The Romance of the Rose for Our Times 13
    Love Song of a Pin-Striped Trouser and a Well-Tailored Jacket 15
    Fair Knights ... A Courtly Love Poem 16
    The Fortune Teller Foresees Her End. 18
    Money, Love, or the Financial Affair 19
    Periodic Table with Hafnium - The Chemistry Must Be Right 21
    How Chaucer Came to My Help in a Dream 22
    Poet at the Poetical Hypermarket 24
    Betrothal: Realism with All Romanticism Removed 26
    Marriage Machine 27

Part 2: Poetic Twerks of Gods and Beasts 29

    And God Created Cat 31
    Pussfluencer - Follow that Cat 32
    Gods Walking Dogs 33
    Bear and Deer 37
    Petocide – A Worryingly Dystopian Poem 39
    Walkies – A Dog Speaks Out 41
    Doggerel - By Teddy, a Springerpoo 42
    The Kelpies: The Water-Horses of Falkirk 43
    All Tied Up – Telephone Answering Machine Messages of the Ancients .. 44
    Behe-Moths 47
    The Trojan War -Three Drafts and a Re-write 48
    Storm Visits Me 52
    The Moon, a Wonder 54
    He Who Sups with the Devil, Needs a Long Spoon 58
    The Sound of Music 60
    Lost in Statistics 61

Part 3: Poetic Twerks on Modern Life and Times 63

    The Scream by Munch (Nordic Noir) 65
    Chains and Circles: The State of the Baltic States. 66
    Malice! Or Who Controls the Trolls? 67
    Seven Deadly Sins 71
    Virtual Holiday from Life 73
    The Queen's Platinum Jubilee 75
    Reimagining King Charles as a Ruthless Shakespearean King 77
    Crafting the Meaning of Life 79

'Hell is Empty – All the Devils are Here'. 81
Assassin Wanted 83
War Dreams 84
Talking Heads 85
The Battle of the Teapots 88
Shakespeare in Space 90
Glass 91
Drama at the Theatre, April 14th, 1865 93
At the Final Trump 94

Part 3: Theatrical Twerks 97

Historic Mini Drama: Napoleon and Josephine 102
Waiting for Godot Act 3 103
Paper, Scissors, Stone – Who has the Last Word? 107
The Trial of God on the Charge of Bad Parenting 109
Fifteen Minutes in the Life of a Honeybee 111
The Post Apocalypse Gin Club 113
Neolithic Knit and Natter 117
Neolithic Tinder Dating, 4000 years B.C. 120
Letters to Sigmund Freud on the Internal Community of Self 122
Herstory: It's the Way You Tell It 125

Part 4: Story Twerks 129

Misunderstood 131
Right Angel, Wrong Virgin 133
Small Words Court Appeal. The Linguistical Hearing 135
Shielded 139
Mental Elf and Safety 141
'Sharing'. A story 144
Love on the Web 146
Cogit-tative Behavioural Therapy 148
The Holiday of a Lifetime 2162 - A Cruise Round Mont Blanc 153
The Dinner Party from Hell 156
Emerging Truth 161
The Nobel Prize for Scientific Creativity 163
On the Brink 165
Random Acts 167
Solitude - Virtually 169
Writers Block - by the Monster itself 172

Foreword

I know what you're thinking: Poetry should be obscure, philosophical, and above all, humourless. Stories and plays should be sharp-edged social observations. But with this collection of absurdities, ironies and linguistical playfulnesses, I am throwing words wildly in the air, and letting them land where I hope to make you smile. They are all written to be read aloud (to yourself, or in public perhaps … but don't get arrested!).

I've had fun with forms and meanings, exploring a range of poetry and prose. But whatever form they appear in, they are all little stories. I love the variety of language we use in daily life, with special forms or registers for different disciplines: science, engineering, music, art, money, politics, and linguistics itself. While one doesn't necessarily need to know the meanings, one can just enjoy the richness of the language, which in the case of science and music, is very evocative and poetic in its own right. You may think I am being abstruse or over wordy exploring these registers, but do not take them too literally or seriously. Just listen to the gist and sound of the imagery. Each has its own unique vocabulary and provides rich pickings for poets. As a nation, we are so language-rich.

I have included some mini-stories, and short sketches too, all of which explore ironies and incongruities, with little twists. I hope you enjoy this kaleidoscope of poems, stories, and sketches. Do not attempt to read them all at once! One or two a week at most. Some are satirical or sinister, but none of them cruelly intended. The grim abstruse stuff will be in my next volume, I promise! (fingers crossed behind my back).

Mary Lister

Part 1: Linguistical Twerks of Life and Love (In Different Registers)

Geography Lovers

(*First included in Trapezing in the Dark, but part of this collection of the Linguistics of Love*)

You are my Far East and my Wild West.
Let's map each other out with our hands,
ride over each other's horizons
with soft-fingered horsemen,
mark out equatorial regions with a survey of kisses,
trace our coastlines and soft lapping shores.

You are my Polar North and my Deep South.
Let's explore our tropics and equators with our lips.
We'll stretch out our longitudes across wild savannahs,
we'll lay our latitudes across wide shores,
and entangle magnetic poles with our limbs.
Take my Mid-Atlantic Ridge, my ravines and rift valleys -
they're yours.
Move my tectonic plates
with earthquakes and magma, in sweet catastrophe.

Fissures and fumaroles flicker with subterranean fire
along our earth bodies and ocean veins.
We are Uranus and Gaia now.
Sky and Earth joined.
You are my geography.
I am your map.

The Tinder Love of the Couch Potatoes

A poignant tale in octava rima (eight-line verse form)

On 'Tinder', swiping idly, you glanced
upon my smiling face and flattering dress.
I was fit, not fat (but digitally enhanced).
You paused and tapped an icon meaning 'YES'.
I'd written that I'd run marathons and danced
(I never mentioned that my life's a mess,
I'd only ever run when running for a bus!).
I never said I was a couch potato – a 'spudo-poto-mus.'

You sent an equal digital untruth,
pictured, padded, paddling a canoe.
I loved the image of adventurous youth,
and clicked the image 'like' and sent it you,
not guessing from the smile, you only had one tooth,
or that you were a couch potato too.
A sofa-surfing lover, far more prone
to addictive gaming on your mobile phone.

We Twitter like lovebirds through each lonesome night.
We 'heart' each other, 'kiss' in every tweet,
glad to hide our true selves out of sight,
and secretly relieved we'll never meet.
I'm your 'lil Miss Perfect', you're my 'Mr Right'.
Our Zoom chemistry is sensuous and sweet.
We'll dine on takeaways, virtually together,
and never need to leave our comfy couches … ever!

Clichés. A Love Song

Hey presto!
It's been an emotional rollercoaster ride,
but at the end of the day … no worries … Awright?

It's raining cats and dogs
But we're sleeping here like logs.
When push comes to shove,
it's a labour of love. No worries … Awright?

Silver linings, blue skies?
The grass is greener on the other side of the fence
if you play your cards right.
It's an uphill battle ... Awright?

Cat got your tongue, got your knickers in a twist?
Airing your dirty laundry?
You can't please everybody,
but ignorance is bliss.

You fit the bill, you're just the ticket,
as the crow flies against all odds.
I won't beat a bird about the bush,
The Old Bull and Bush (da da dadada).

More haste, less rush,
bite the hand that bites the dust.
Take the bull by the horns,
and put the cart before the horse.

Whoa! Hold your horses!
Don't put that cart before that horse!
Don't look that gift horse in the mouth!
Don't flog this dead horse of a different colour.

It's the hair of a dog, so let sleeping dogs lie.
You green-eyed monster you,
killing two birds with one stone.
Nothing to sneeze at, not in my backyard.

Pig in a poke, it's no joke.
You and your red herrings, slippery as eels,
thick as thieves, up to your ears.
What goes around comes around ... Awright?

It's been an emotional rollercoaster,
but at the end of the day, with the wolf at the door,
words fail me, no worries!
You're too hot to handle, I can't hold a candle.

End of story ... Awright?

Revelations in Soap Operas

Revelations intertwine
in each soap opera storyline:
That someone's father's cousin's son
shot your sister with a gun,
and someone else's brother's wife
stabbed What-d'you-call-him with a knife.
And Thingy's boyfriend's cousin's dad,
with an axe went raving mad
at a wedding in the Vic,
while someone else's son was sick.

Old Jim served porridge many times,
for his unmentionable crimes.
But he's released, so please watch out
for GBH when he's about.
That man who moved to Number 8
looks psychotic. Do not wait …
He's into the dark web and the dark arts
- check out his fridge for body parts!

Your neighbours thought it right and fair
t'hold dogging nights in Albert Square.
It brought the community together
to goggle watch in any weather!
Your senile grandma had a fling
and ran a lewd sex-trafficking ring,
revealing too, your Ma and Pop
kept a secret knocking shop.
Your auntie fought a long hard fight
with 'cancer' and with 'failing sight,'
revealing at her final breath
that *Syphilis* had caused her death.

Your kids at high school need extolling
for international spin and trolling.

They put their mobile phones to use
in underage porn and sex abuse.

The Woolpack is the rendezvous
of Russian poisoners … more than two.
They smear each farmer's door and lock
with silage mixed with Novichok.
And DNA has now revealed,
a new contender in the field -
your lover's dad donated sperms
to all girls in t' Rovers' Returns.
Your wife's in fact your sister, it confirms.

But now I must reveal to you:
You're just a '*character*'- not *real* or *true*!
You're only glamorous and exciting
in some scriptwriter's lurid writing.
This revelation leaves no hope …
soap operas use carbolic soap!

Musical Passion

(To be read in a suggestive Italian accent. No need to know the musical terms!)

They were a *symphony,*
with a *libretto* and many movements.
He, *baritone basso*, and blowing his own trumpet
with *largamente sforzando* and *brusquemento* embrasure.
She, *mezzo soprano*, all *vibrato* and *tremulo vivaci.*
It started as a *rubato* rhapsody, *ma non-troppo,*
- a mere *pizzicato* in a café rouge,
but swiftly *arpeggio*-ed through *ostinato*
into a *scherzo forte* off the scale.
At first, *adagio andante* and *de capo.*
He, double-cleffed in full *cadenza, crescendo.*
She, more *adagio*, in *glissando* motif.
Together, *fortepiano*, (sometimes flat but ... always sharp).
Perhaps he was too *brusquecante,* too *dal segno* in the brass section.
Maybe her *giacosa* was too *sfogato* on her *viola de gamba*?

Perhaps some *maestro* was tickling their ivories,
plucking their strings, orchestrating their arias,
notating their every movement,
predicting their final *cadenza,*
as they moved *con sordino*, from *cadence* to catastrophe,
rallentando al fini?
It was he, *falsetto, forte, mezzo forte*, thundering full pedal,
that led to the great *crescendo*, the end of the canon.
And she*, retardando, staccato coloratura,*
Shrieked her last *fermata trill coda,*
and ran off with a counter tenor *accelerando.*
Final chord. *Castrato! Fini!*
No more cornettoes!

Last Tango in Orpington

(An attempt at a non-binary linguistic romance. The poet wrestles with the new pronouns. No offence intended.)

They saw Them across the ballroom floor.
Ze took Xe in Their inclusive arms
and whispered in Their ear, "on t'adore!"
Xe succumbed to Ze's gender-neutral charms.

It was a wild but short-lived true romance.
Non-binary in every spoken word,
fluidity in each step, each dance
yet not beyond linguistically absurd.

Tongue-tied, each sentence that They spoke,
became a puzzle for Their poet's mind,
as de-identifying bird and bloke
a whole new vocab has to be defined!

"It's a linguistic nightmare!" They observed.
"Better say Night-*gelding!* - *Mare* is such a gendered thing."
"This learning curve is far too steeply curved."
"But then *Curve* is quite suggestive ... has a female ring."

They waltzed with unbridled passion,
embodying non-verbally, all amorous arts
de-sexed the foxtrot, in gender-fluid fashion,
embraced pansexual leanings of Their hearts.

At last, in Orpington, the Tango was Their great undoing.
The highly gendered nature of the dance fell flat.
Who was to lead or follow, was a heterosexist question!
Neither was willing to be mis-gendered,

They left the ballroom in disgust,
– and That ... They agreed ... was That!

A Medieval Nightmare: The Romance of the Rose for Our Times

(This is a modern version of the Classic medieval French poem 'Le Roman de la Rose' by Guillaume de Lorris and Jean de Meun. In my version, Rose is a drug addict – very far from the courtly love tradition, and the garden is a chatroom on the dark web. Spoiler Alert: A happy ending, nevertheless!)

It must have been the Nytol, cos I fell into a daze,
and dreamt a dream to startle and amaze.
There was a gate, and over it was written:
"Enter this Virtual Chatroom for the Dead or Smitten".
As I approached, the gates then opened wide,
and I could see a hydroponic garden there inside,
where cannabis and poppies grow
in artificial light from seeds, the dealers sow.

In the centre stood a darkly hooded man.
"Welcome to my chatroom. Click 'unmute' if you can.
Here is Lady Fortune, here's Disaster …
And here is Death, your chatroom host and master.
And here," he gestured, "is the Lady Rose –
casualty from the last Love Island I suppose."
Lady Fortune spoke, "Why are you here?
Why this chatroom when you could be anywhere?
If Chance is what you want, then take a chance,
and ask the Lady Rose to dance with you her last most fatal dance."

Disaster intervened, "I summoned him to come,
to court disaster and make Pandemonium."
Death held up his hand, and Silence fell.
"This is the game, to rescue Rose from drug-addicted Hell.
Here she is merely virtual, only seen on Zoom.
The real Rose lies dying in some derelict room
of Ketamine and Coke, and other drugs beside.
Go find her if you dare. Make her your deathly bride."

Dear Reader, some one thousand lines must pass
before my tale is fully told at last…
or leave it to Jean de Meun to end the story,
promoting it from Nightmare into Glory.
I challenged Lady Fortune, gambled with Disaster,
rescued my Lady Rose from Death, her master.
On Tinder and in chatrooms round the world,
the tenderest of heroic loves unfold.
Me and my drug-addicted lover, Lady Rose,
live happily in a council flat in Ladbroke Grove.

Love Song of a Pin-Striped Trouser and a Well-Tailored Jacket

(Inspired by a production by IOU Theatre in the Yorkshire Sculpture Park)

JACKET
    You seem like a colossus
    as you stride across the mill.
    My inside pocket quavered
    and my warp and weft stood still.
    But I knew we were compatible,
    Cut from the same cloth,
    Oh, dart into my tailored arms,
    safe from time and moth.

TROUSERS
    Your buttons seemed to jigger mine.
    They spoke of be-spoke treasure.
    My inside leg was tremulous
    as I took your measure.
    Our pinstripes seem a likely match –
    We're worsteds of a feather.
    We're of one hank, one spool, one batch.
    Yes! We belong together.

BOTH
    Yes ... together we are intertwined.
    No trouser should be single.
    It suits us to co-ordinate,
    to join our seams and mingle.
    Zipped up, with our sartorial charms,
    we'll stride down Saville Row,
    and pose with double breasted arms,
    united in one fashion show.

"Here be Dragons" by Polly Walker

Fair Knights … A Courtly Love Poem

(In the courtly love tradition, ladies set seemingly impossible tasks for knights to perform. Very few survived!)

"Fair knights on snorting, snaffling steeds
underneath my tower,
first perform me daring deeds
and I will throw you roses from my window-box-ed bower.
Bring me claw of Chimaera,
and griffin horn from Nineveh,
and newborn baby dragon down
from which to weave a wedding gown.
Then, aspicked hoof of unicorn,
some diamonds of the cosmos' dawn
a phoenix egg to breakfast on,
a hydra's head … or two …
and if by then you're still not dead,
I'll swear to love you true!

We'll build a castle in the clouds,
beneath the setting sun.
And all day I will sing to you
of bygone kings, and things
that other bygone knights have done.
And I will rub your armour bright
with sunflower pads and nectarite,
bathe you in ambrosia dew,
cook you some sea-serpent stew,
tickle you with peacock wings,
conceive a dynasty of kings,
knit you vests of gossamer thread,
and kiss you in a dahlia bed.
Yes! I will be your fairy wife,
in happy-ever-afterlife … If you are not DEAD!

The Fortune Teller Foresees Her End.

(In Pushkin's 14 line 'Onegin' stanzas, on the theme of the Tarot, inspired by Charles William's novel, the 'Greater Trumps'. The names and pictures of the Tarot cards are very evocative, but detailed notes are not necessary to understand the poem.)

Her eyes take in the tarot at one glance.
Two stark cards have struck their deafening chords.
The High Priestess plays the game of chance,
and piercing her own heart, the Three of Swords.
She deals the cards again and finds the falling Tower.
Again, again, the Emperor and the Devil fight for power.
The Ace of Pentacles now deals another blow:
six cards portending death, within a single row.
Her trembling hand the Great Arcana turns.
Now the Moon breathes incipient fears of madness
across subconscious realms of sadness.
And here the Wheel of Fortune, blazing … burns.
She sees the portents of the tarot laid out clear.
Self-prophecy of lonely death within a year.

She drew her dagger from its velvet sheath
and thrust its point against her upturned throat.
She must fulfil the dreadful prophecy she read beneath,
however cabalistic, ancient or remote.
But suddenly the pack of tarots rose
into a rainbow arch across the room and froze.
Down stepped the Fool, bearing in his hands
the Ace of Cups with water flowing across barren lands,
the Queen of Swords with pentacles and flowers.
The Knight of Wands, Lord of Lightning and of Flame
swore she was the Princess of the Echoing Hills again.
Then the Magician used his great hermetic powers
to end this glimpse into the chaos of all things,
that glance into the known unknowable, the tarot brings.

Money, Love, or the Financial Affair

Lead me to the land of milk and money
where the cash flows fast and deep.
We can climb the money mountains -
where pennies drop from heaven in a heap.

We'll invest in fiscal forests,
and shake the money trees,
in Autumn's frozen assets
and Winter's liquidity-freeze.

Oh, the banks are flocked with brokers
waiting for the gravy boat
to cross troubled financial waters
where hard currencies can't float.

There, arcane financial wizards
wear investments of fool's gold,
wrought by profiteers of bankruptcy
from gross profits bought and sold.

Let's share a beer in a bear market
and hold a quarterly review
in a quiet and cool recession
take a fiscal risk or two.

Let us balance on gross margins,
sing monthly statements in invoice,
do acrobatics in accounting,
create accruals of our choice.

We'll trip the fraudulent fantastic
in an asset-stripping dance,
and gamble in bull markets
in gazumping games of chance.

Though money cannot 'buy us love',
the financial future's fine.
We will roast the Root of Evil,
drink fluidity and wine!

I'll grab your tangible assets
and the money will be mine.
For, its money makes the world go round,
and music to my ears
is the clink of cash and coinage.
- It's the music of the spheres!

Periodic Table with Hafnium - The Chemistry Must Be Right ...

(The periodic table in this poem is just an idea for a restaurant table where a couple meet. You don't need to understand any of the terms. They are all actual scientific terms, but just enjoy the suggestibility of the words)

Come let us sit at the *Periodic Table*, you, and I,
silhouetted by the vast and elemental sky.
You can discuss your rather *Tensile Strength*,
while I can thrill you with my *Viscosity* at length.
You might divulge your *Molar Heat Capacity*,
and I discuss my *Enthalpy* with vivacity.
Pre-prandials of *Hafnium* are served from an *Isobar*.
We'll sip *Oxidated Helium* cocktails from a glass bell jar.
Our hors d'oeuvres is *Copernicum,* served in a *petri dish.*
Our entrée is *Seaborgian Poisson Ratio* ... a kind of fish,
served with *Lattice Angles*, cooked *en croute*.
For dessert, some *Ductile Fluoride* from a *Bunsen flute*.

But, if you exercise your *Critical Atomic Weight*,
I will *entropically* change my *chemical state*.
You're *paramagnetic* ... I often tell you so.
But sometimes my *Electronic Conductivity* is very, very low.
Your *Boiling Point* is sometimes hard to gauge.
Your *Ionising Energies* put you in an elemental rage.
And even though you are my *exothermic* hero,
my *Melting Point* can veer from *Fahrenheit* to *Celsius Zero*.
And if my *Covalent Radius* and my *Modal Bulk*
need *Elasticity* to expand my *radial hulk*,
then please forgive these trembling *isotopes,*
and put it down to *thermal Allotropes*!
It may be only *Periodically* we meet,
but oh, this *alchemy* is so, so sweet!
And if we get the *Chemistry* right ...
let's book this *Periodic Table* for another night!

How Chaucer Came to My Help in a Dream

(The imperious King who demands a story is Richard II, who, in Shakespeare's play, says: 'Come, let us sit upon the ground, and tell sad stories of the death of Kings'. He was King in Chaucer's day)

One day as I sat beneath my rowan tree,
an opiate drowsiness came over me.
I dreamt that I was standing at a door,
within my garden walls, I'd never seen before.
And round my neck, I found a golden key.

It opened into a medieval hall,
and at the table head, a King, regal and tall.
Beside him, Chaucer sat. He beckoned me to sit,
(I felt extremely shy I must admit),
but walked the table length, past courtiers all.

Chaucer whispered to me that I was late.
They'd had long centuries to sit and wait
to hear my story, which I now must tell
to amuse the gathered company - and tell it well,
though yet unwritten, as in dreams often is one's fate.

I, somewhat panicked, curtseyed to the King,
and bowed to courtiers, trying to find something,
some story, mystery, tale, or anecdote,
some poem learned long ago by rote…
My mind went blank. My inner bard went PING!

"I … er … know no tales!" The King threw down his cup.
"If you can't remember, you must make one up!"
My tears flowed freely down my face,
when Chaucer, kindly sensing my disgrace,
slid me a scroll with writing at the top.

God knows how I read his story there!
But when I finished, they all stood to cheer.
The story was a wonder, beautiful and gripping,
full of thwarted love and joyous bodice-ripping.
I'd found my voice and told his story loud and clear.

If only I could have memorised that tale
told in my dream, I know I would not fail
to ever galvanise my gathered audience
with thoughts of love, of mystery and suspense …
But dreams come to an end and all my memories pale –
except that Chaucer saved me from a medieval gaol!

Poet at the Poetical Hypermarket

I took my dear friend 'the Poet',
who suffered from writer's block,
to a huge hypermarket of verbiage,
to replenish his poetic stock.

The shop had a lit-up sign 'Metaphorz',
(No doggerels permitted inside).
There were aisles of poetic linguistics,
and trolleys a quatrain wide.

He was off on his trolley, triumphant,
excited by all that he saw.
Shelves stacked high as Babylon's towers,
up to the ceilings and down to the floor.

One aisle had debates and didactics,
dialogues, prologues, and prose,
prosodies, pastiche, and plagiarisms,
all in postmodernist rows.

Another had specialist lyrics,
allegories, elegies, 'flarfs',
pentameters, hexameters, dactyls ...
enjambments, ellipses (for laughs.)

There were epics, acrostics and sapphics,
elegies, pantoums and odes,
canzones, and cantos and concepts,
terza rimas, and trochees in loads.

On aisle 4 were displayed all the archetypes ...
images, symbols, and genres.
at least seven allowed ambiguities,
with a wide range of double-entendres.

Arranged in small boxes marked 2-for-1 offers,
were structures and stresses, and tenses and tones,
concepts and couplets, metres and motifs,
labials, lexicons and of course ... allophones.

A spurious Thesaurian chorus
offered discounts on certain semantics,
spiced with alliterative fricatives,
labials, glottals and graphic romantics.

Litotes, and litanies, lyrical ballads,
haikus and tercets, and villanelles wild.
elegies, epigrams, bucolic heroics ...
My Poet was stuffing his face like a child!

His trolley was tottering, unstoppably toppling
piled high with lexical booty upon it.
But he fatally paused at the very last aisle,
marked 'Shakespearian and Petrarchan sonnet'.

The final last straw for his tottering trolley
was the end rhyming couplet which sums up the thought.
The whole thing fell sideways and smashed into phonemes,
 ... so, all inspiration amounted to nought.

He fell on the floor and snatched to catch concepts.
They ellipsed his grasp, he strophed at the shock.
The lights went out sharply. 'The Metaphorz' shut.
So, my Poet returned to his old Writers' block.

The moral of this story is - don't be an oxymoron. One poem at a time and go gently on the forms and metres.

Betrothal: Realism with All Romanticism Removed

Take me, and all that I own is yours, beloved,
for better or worse, for richer or poorer.
With my body I will thee worship.
All my worldly goods I will thee endow.
Including the following: -
My family, my aging parents, mostly whingeing
always bickering,
plus, my dysfunctional siblings, especially my alcoholic
brother,
and my seriously drug-addicted sister,
a lorryload of cousins, who visit often,
a smattering of eccentric and demanding aunts,
and a very needy relative always beseeching financial help.
(Nobody knows how she is related, or whether at all,
but she always comes for Christmas.)
Also, part of the deal is:
My unpaid student loans going back a decade,
debts from my various credit cards,
(I went AWOL in the noughties)
a court order for unpaid rentals,
a vet bill from my incontinent slightly pointless poodle,
and a few garage bills from my ageing Cortina.

So, let's drink a glass of champagne
and live happily ever after,
sharing in all bodily sickness and mental health,
(Did I mention my psychiatrist's bills?)
till Death us do part.
And don't even get me started on YOUR dysfunctional
family … they'll be the death of me!
Bottoms up! Up yours forever!
When is the wedding did you say?

Marriage Machine

(A love song in engineering-speak)

We've been married so long.
We should be a well-oiled machine by now.
The chemistry is still there. What about the physics?
We are twin engines
powering towards some distant destination,
galvanised, structural components still operational.
The tracks are well-laid,
the magnetic bonding still intact,
the multi-bodied systems well buffered,
the sum of our parts seems co-efficient.

But on closer structural analysis,
the wheel axles are rusting,
our sprockets are unsynchronised,
some of our levers are experiencing gravitational pull.
Our gauge pressures are variable,
our belt chains are expanding,
our tensile strength diminishing,
our turbines are on different trajectories,
the hydraulics are creaking,
and our linkages experience stress.

There are moments of mass inertia. Let's enjoy them.
Pour the champagne to oil our mechanisms.
Defy those laws of thermodynamics!
Let's put our feet up after our long-mechanised journey
through the ferromagnetic fields of life.

We should settle into the gentle siding of old age,
our engines gently combusting with an almost silent hiss,
into poetry, without motion.

Part 2: Poetic Twerks of Gods and Beasts

And God Created Cat

Out of Darkness came a whispered "Miaow",
then a reverberating "YEOWL!" across the Universe.
And the Great Cat-God ... became!
On the first day, he created Earth and cat litter.
On the second day, he invented fish and Catastrophes.
On the third day, he made cushions and Catechisms.
On the fourth day, worm pills and Cat-a-Nine-Tails.
On the fifth day, cat flaps, and Cat-a-Meringues.
On the sixth day, he created Whiskers, Purina and
categorical feline fishy pamper-treats.
But, on day seven he created Cat.
And God saw that Cat was good, verrrrrrrry verrrrrrrry good.
So, the Almighty purred, and dozed catatonic on cushions
until dinner was served in a silver bowl marked God-Puss
(which he shared with the Goddess Bastet... without
caterwaul).

And that, my dears, was CAT!

Pussfluencer - Follow that Cat

(Some cats earn huge amounts of money on social media, promoting a wide range of products)

I am the cat that used to "Walk by Itself."
But now I have a million followers.
I am Madame Fluffsky, furry-tailed Purrshun Blue.
Pussfluencer, influencer, prrrroper cata-geezer.
Click-a-cat-bait.
All eyes are turned on me, mouse eyes, beyond screens,
as I pounce prettily, or purr fatly, fuzzily in the catmint bed …

Or my purrrrsonal favourite, opening the frrrridge door
with my paw
to swipe some fishy treats,
She sets up fluffy birds on wires, so I dance prrrettily,
strrrrictly celebrrricat. It's a click-a-thon.
Or she knits woolly balls aka mice, so I pounce, tiger-cat,
Clickety-click. #FunnyKitten. Miaow-miaow mode.

I pat-paw the fishbowl, goldfish clickbait,
though my preference is (apparently) a vegan fish
casserrrole served in a diamante bowl.
I can recommend a good vet, at a prrrrice,
and why not rrrrrreal estate, prrrrivate healthcare,
and a 5-star crrrrrruise?

I strrrretch luxuriously in my fur-lined basket,
yowling RRRRRossini's Cat Duet softly, (both parts),
Mihihi hihihi miaOW!
or doze catatonic in catnap.
I am Bastet, with a million followers.
Prrractically a goddess already.
#Click-a-Cat #Pussfluencer

Gods Walking Dogs

(In myths they really do have dogs)

Now, nobody knows, but I'm telling you now,
that once a year on New Year's Day,
the gods come down from their high-flown clouds,
and the dogs of the gods get to play.

They descend to the place they call Ragnarök Park
with their Cruftian-hounds on titanic leads.
The dogs love their 'walkies' and all start to bark,
and the Annual God-Dog Day proceeds.

There is Goddess Kali with waving arms,
and her long-tongued manicured bitches.
But the Goddess of Death gets quite out of breath
as they doggedly run through the muddiest ditches.

Tichzicatl, Aztec god of Storms,
has Ahuizotl who takes many forms.
He throws up a ball or a stick to this cur,
and his stickle-back prickles become fluffy fur.

Now Loki the Trickster has a hellhound,
called Fenry, who howls with a blood-curling sound.
He has burning red eyes and huge snarling lips.
When he growls, it incurs the APOCALYPSE!

Assyrian Marduk with huge, feathered wings,
has a winged spotted dog on a chain.
But the dog has bad habits, a penchant for rabbits.
When he runs, he precipitates rain!

The Goddess Athena has a pooch called Irena.
Alongside walk Zeus and Hecate
with three-headed Cerberus, on a long leash,
next, come the Sphinx and Astarte.

The Japanese God of storms, Sushanoo,
has a hurricane hound called Ignami.
Let him loose? He won't risk it, bribes the dog with a biscuit.
But he only responds to salami.

Then Thetis and Sedna rise up from the lake
lead by a serpent and fish.
Innumerable hounds making blood-curdling sounds
run amok from a local abyss …

There is Amarok, Aralez, Barghest and Kludde,
Geri, and Feki, Psoglav and Skoll,
Gwligi, Gamr, and Gelert and Yeth,
lie down in the mud and have a good roll.

"Walkies!" shouts Isis in dread Judgement Halls,
Anubis bounds up to her doggerel calls.
A walk in the park, a pee and a bark,
and good sniff at other dogs' balls.

It's a glorious pedigree dog show indeed.
Bum-sniffing, bones buried, tails up.

There is snarling and growling and yelping and howling,
dating and mating, begetting of pup.

When the Great Barking stops, at the end of the day,
each god calls its dog and leads it away
to celestial or bestial kennels sublime
till the next New Year's Day God-Dog Walkies time.

But this year the whole thing went terribly wrong.
A trickster-god jokingly sounded a gong.
The gods thought it really was the 'APOCALYPSE',
and they panicked the dogs with whistles and whips.

Each god grabbed the wrong dog, and whisked it away,
flew back to their kingdoms in North, West and East,
and this chaos and panic caused canine dismay,
With the dire separation of God, pooch and beast.
The Hellhounds are howling and shaking the skies,
the Fire-Dogs are furious and temperatures rise.
Climate disaster was forged from their rage,
and we need a new dog walk to turn a new page.

We can only hope that the peace is restored,
and each dog is returned to its goddess or lord.
This canine catastrophe's caused worldwide grief.
Let's hope the next God-Dog Walk will bring some relief!

Taking Care

"Let me take good care of you,"
said Tiger to the care-worn Hare.
"You must come home and rest with me,
In the luxury of my lair."
The careless Hare was dazzled
in the headlights of his eyes.
She rode the Tiger to his den,
completely hypnotised.

"Just pop into that cooking pot …
it makes a comfy bed.
I take good care of all my guests."
The caring Tiger carelessly said.
"Now, a soft and pillowy onion,
plus, juniper, I think.
And a blanket of rich gravy!"
He said with a tigerish wink.

She saw the care-free tiger cubs,
each nursed a stripey plate.
"Oh no! I don't need care right now …
I think I'd rather wait!"
Too Late! The Tiger pounced on her.
Through gritted teeth growled he,
"I SAID I would take care of you,
and I CARE about my tea!"

"You're taking care of dinner!"
You're such a caring Dad!"
The tiger cubs purred proudly …
The care-worn Hare looked sad.
The moral of this story
is to read between the lines,
or read between the Tiger's stripes,
and TAKE CARE at all times!

Bear and Deer

Deer was the sweetest creature in the dark forest.
She sipped from streams and glided
graceful through dappled shadows, she weaved,
nibbling on fronded leaves,
barely seen or spied.

But there was one thing that threatened her,
It was Bear, huge and hoary.
Eater of forest creatures,
grim with hairy features
fierce and gory.

He caught Deer in his frightful claws
and growled that here and now
he would tear Deer's fur
and eat her flesh
while still tender and still fresh.

Then Deer cried out to Moon, to forest, and to trees.
Moon stepped down with soft and silvery glow.
"Trees, all gather round. Hold Bear down.
Wait till Dawn rises with the Sun.
Wait Deer, and the birds will come."

Trees' snaking arms held Bear fast.
He growled and struggled to break free.
He bit and scratched, and scraped the bark
of every twining branch
and every twisting trunk of tree.

When the first candlelight of Dawn lit up the sky,
flocks of tiny birds flew down,
and settled on Deer's antlers high.
They sang a song of sorrow, loss, and war,
with a sweet haunting sadness never heard before.

Bear listened and his cruel eyes glistened.
A tear rolled down his hoary face.
Tears fell in rivers, fell in streams.
turning him to crystal ice,
into a frozen statue, locked in grizzly dreams.

Now the crystal Bear stands tall
in the forest clearing, not threatening at all to passers-by.
Frozen into ice with his own tears.
Never more a danger to forest folk or deers.
The power of birdsong to transform, transmogrify!

Petocide – A Worryingly Dystopian Poem

The Government cooked up some reasons:
Pets were divisive, 'anti-green!'
They wanted a 'Lockdown of National Joys',
so, replacing each pet with mechanical toys,
or 'robo-pets' seemed like a dream.

It wasn't about the cutting of carbon,
but the cutting of national pleasure.
So, to lower emissions
of puppies and kittens
seemed a totally reasonable measure.

"Pets are heavy on carbon: they gobble up meat.
They whine and they pee, and they poo.
Let's put all pets down,
or run out of town,
to a great abattoir, in a queue?"

They created a brand-new post of 'Pet Tsar'.
The perks were enormous of course.
Ten grand for a poodle beloved of the nation,
five grand for a Bulldog, a Peke or Alsatian,
and twenty-five grand for a horse.

Soon came the ominous bang on each door.
Van loads of pets were driven away.
Sounds of barking and growling,
of miaowing and howling,
haunted the streets night and day.

The Pet Tsar claimed to be cutting-edge 'Green'
with the pace of the 'Petocide' vast and obscene.
"The cows are still farting
so, we must be parting
with cattle - so no more butter or cream."

Then the policy took off around the whole world.
They rounded up elephants, zebra and deer.
And as for the zoos,
they were emptied in twos,
like Noah's Ark, backwards, I fear.

Our planet was emptied of wildlife and pets.
Then governments went overboard.
They built factories to churn out
Tamagotchis – so Burnout! -
gross global emissions seriously soared!

All ended in tears as you well may have guessed.
Mega-factories turned blue skies to black.
"Let's bring back the pets!"
But the Pet Tsar regrets,
"It's too late, and there's no turning back!"

So, the Great Mass Extinction was started by Man.
But mankind was choked in the fumes
of abattoirs burning,
and factories churning …
So, our world WAS by carbon, completely consumed!

Walkies – A Dog Speaks Out

The front door opens at last!
It's like Beethoven's Ninth to us dogs
and a glorious hologram in five dimensions of SMELL.
I choke on my lead, leaping into a Shangri-La of scent.
I sniff a million-layered history of Dog.
It's archaeology in nasal form ... whiffs eternal!

But who is this hauling me
from the Litter Bin of Celestial Snuff?
It's my two-legged Dog Walker and Nosh Provider.
She means well but has a handicap, poor dear.
A one-dimensional nose. i.e., L N I ...
Limited Nasal Intelligence.
She calls 'Walkies' thinking only of some dreary trudge
to the end of the road and back,
completely ignorant of the multiverse I blissfully explore,
my leg-cocking paradise!

I woof, snuffle, and scrabble and scruffle the dead leaves
for the Meaning of Whiff,
for some message from the Great Dog,
The Canine Omnipresence.
And you know what? The Meaning of Whiff is SMELL,
is quivering noses, nasal earthy delights,
is the multiverse of rhinal intelligence.
Dogverse. Poetry on four paws.

The front door bangs shut behind us.
The only smell is Dettol and air freshener.
I am back in three dimensions like a blackout.
Walkies snuffed out. Like a candle.

Doggerel - By Teddy, a Springerpoo

(In Arf, with translation)

Arrrrrr Grrrh Gerrrrhah
One joyous bound
Arrrrafff. Arrrf arrf!
Arrif arrafffah! Arrrh!
I leap into the Smelliverse.
Arrraf Grrrrharf Arif Arrrrraf
My nose sniffs all around.
Arrrgerragrrrh
I find I have to take to verse.
Arrraf araf Graff Gruff Arf
My poetry could not be worse!

Grrrrrarf gruff grrrh arf
Smells, everywhere I sniff.
Arriff riff ruff grrrarf.
In the Smelliverse divine.
Arfff araf ggrrrarrr!
Some scents are slightly miff ...
Grrrh!
Each piddle is a text or sign.
ArrrrrrrH Grrr arfrf
A love letter in whiff ...
Arrf rrrrrrgrrrr araf arf aarf araf
WOOF!

The Kelpies: The Water-Horses of Falkirk

They erupt from motorway and canal,
these silver-headed Kelpies, reborn.
They are the shapeshifting water-horses of Scottish lochs
and legends, who appear as men,
then, in a sudden flash,
morph into horse-headed monsters of the deep
to tear the flesh of unwary women
before they can leap to safety over running water.
These Kelpies are caught in time,
as they break out from distant myth.
One holds its head high, freeing its bonds,
aspiring to fly from dark centuries in children's tales.
The other, head lowered,
gathers power in haunches still underground,
holding back its speed for the big leap upwards.
In the canal there are only still waters, not running.
No white horses or waves, no rivers, no seas.
No sanctuary then from these wild unchained forces.
Beautiful and terrible, miracles of engineering,
they fly upwards from Scotland's reimagined roots
deep in the granite earth,
re-mystified, re-mythed
into a brave new futuristic world.

All Tied Up – Telephone Answering Machine Messages of the Ancients

(All the mythic and historical characters below were famously tied up – and couldn't get to their phones – perhaps!)

Brrrring Brrrring!
Prometheus here. I can't speak right now.
I'm all tied up
 ... to a precipice in the high Caucasus,
And these nasty birds of prey are forever pecking at my liver ...
If you're phoning for our RSPB Eagle-Watch programme
Press 3.
If you want our God to Mortal chat line
Press 5.
For all other services leave a message after the ... groan.

Brrrring Brrrring!
Hello. Andromeda here.
I can't speak right now.
I'm all tied up ... to a massive rock,
expecting a virgin-eating sea-dragon shortly.
Hopefully Perseus will arrive by flying horse
to rescue me just in time
from Poseidon's spiteful wife.
Why did mummy open her big bragging mouth?
I can't help being pretty!
For mother/daughter matricide advice,
Press1
If you are enquiring about our Reptile Rescue Service,
Press 2
For all other services leave a message after the long moan.

Brrrring! Brrrring!
Odysseus here, Hero/Trickster Incorporated.
I can't answer your call right now,
as I'm all tied up to a mast,
listening to a choir of salty bints trying to allure me

with some sales patter about prime real estate
on their body-strewn island.
Judging by the bones round their fishy tales,
it's a fools' graveyard.
Please leave a message in mesmerising song.
If you are enquiring about our Siren Holiday homes
Press 2. You are customer one million, four thousand, nine hundred and seventy-three,
So, try not to listen to the alluring muzak.

Brrrring! Brrrring!
Joan of Arc speaking.
I can't take your call just now.
I am a bit tied up to a stake. Ze Bloody English
are lighting torches and calling moi 'ze French 'arlot'.
Soon I will be, 'ow d'you say? ... Toast? Croissant? Croque Monsieur?
In the unlikely event of a Divine Intervention,
I will return your call.
If you are enquiring about post-Brexit French Visa service,
Press 1
For ze 'Undred Years War re-enactment dates and times,
Press 2
If you are replying to our Quiz question "Where ze 'ell is Arc?", Press 3
For all ozzer services, press every button in sight
Après ze piercing scream ... !

Brrrrimg! Brrrring!
Guy Fawkes and his merry men speaking.
Can't speak to you right now …
We're all tied up
and ready for the Contravention of Fire Regulations Event.
For enquiries about new draconian anti-terrorist measures,
Press 1
For hanging, drawing and quartering counselling services
please ring King James the First on our helpline.

If you are an extreme Catholic, and need advice on keeping your head, and other body parts,
Press 3
For expressions of sympathy,
please leave a message after the whimper
and I won't get back to you anytime soon.
(Flat tone ...)

Behe-Moths

Soft fluttering velvet moths love nothing better
than the comfort fodder of one's mohair sweater.
They flit in innocently to hunker down
for winter, wrapped in fleecy eiderdown.

Soft moths chew slow with velveteen jaws
the fluffy fabric in one's bottom drawers.
Lay mothling eggs and larva fatly swelling,
munching with minute mincing teeth,
the carpets of one's dwelling.

Come Spring, the fabric of our lives is all undone!
Our home's one mighty moth-work, lacey and un-spun.
Hell-bent as locust, munching to line its nest.
Passive-aggressive foe … a Behe-moth! ... A pest!

The Trojan War -Three Drafts and a Re-write

(Homer was not the only bard to write about the Trojan War. There were other lost epics. In this poem, Stasinus and Arctinus were actual poets, while Demodocus was the fictional bard in Homer's Odyssey, who sings about the Trojan War, moving Odysseus to tears)

Silence fell on the banquet, and the King proclaimed:
"Three Bards will sing of the Trojans and Greeks,
and each bard will be named.
Step forward Stasinus, bard of the Cypria."
A blind bard stepped up on the plinth
and skilfully struck his lyre, hoping to set their hearts on fire.
"I sing of the Judgement of Paris,
of the three goddesses, Hera, Athene and Aphrodite."

(He coughed and cleared his throat.)

"Aphrodite offered Love."

(And here he struck a note)

"Hera offered him Power."

(he struck a discord on his strings)

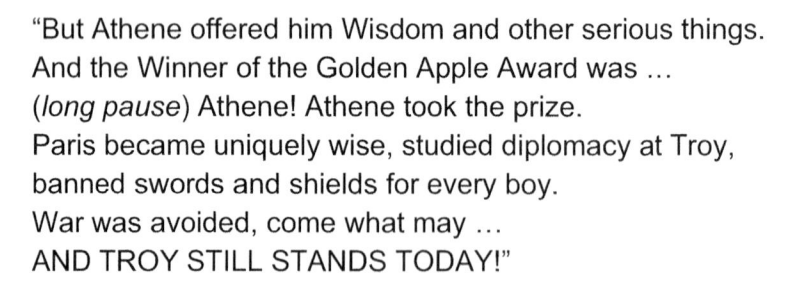

"But Athene offered him Wisdom and other serious things.
And the Winner of the Golden Apple Award was …
(*long pause*) Athene! Athene took the prize.
Paris became uniquely wise, studied diplomacy at Troy,
banned swords and shields for every boy.
War was avoided, come what may …
AND TROY STILL STANDS TODAY!"

(There was a short pause, then disappointed clapping.)

"And now," said the King. "Step forward,
Bard number two, Arctinus of Miletus.
Give him a big Greek hand and let him greet us!"
Arctinus took his stand with lyre in hand.
"I sing of the minor annoyance of Achilles.

He was a bit miffed.
And Agamemnon was slightly annoyed too, and a little sad,
to have to return his mistress Chryseis to her dad.
But decided to send for his own wife
Clytemnestra, thus avoiding Aegisthus' bloody knife."

(*The audience looked bored stiff*)

"Peace was achieved, and everyone
shook hands,
AND TO THIS VERY DAY TROY
STANDS!"

(*Someone in the audience started
clapping but stopped when no one else did*).

The King said, "Moving on, to the climax of this epic tale,
Demodocus, bard number three, all hail!"
Demodocus strung his lyre and swiftly played,
the culmination and catharsis couldn't be delayed.
"I sing of the Wooden Trojan Horse
built on the beaches where the Greeks were camped.
Five mighty trees were felled as a resource,
and the horse rose up on wooden ramps.
Then, after many days of quiet debate,
the Trojans dragged it up to Troy's own gate.
But lack of nails made the whole structure sway.
The flimsy girders tottered and fell away.
Out fell the Greeks to certain slaughter,
so never rescued Helen, Leda's naughty daughter.
AND TROY STILL STANDS TODAY!"

(*Final strumming, but no one clapped*)

"Is that all?" someone whispered. "Nothing sad?
No guts in t'dust?" No one going mad with lust?"
"I would have liked a bit of sacking!"
"A bit of hacking would be cracking!"
The audience began to shout.

But Homer, taking notes throughout,
wrote, "I sing of **madness** and the
bloody tale of **war** …"
And he put in **a lot more** gore!
It read much better than before,
wild poetry and Homeric metaphor ...
what's not to love?
The audience seemed to like it more.
Us modern bards should learn a lesson:
More blood, more gore, if you want to impress 'em!

Trees Dance

SSSShhh! It's a secret.
Trees dance. Yes! When no one is looking …
In the half light of dusk
or the misty moonlight of a waning moon.
Yes, when the wind blows, it's their turn to start.

Arms up, entwining branches,
enmeshing twigs, swaying trunks - sometimes
with fat-bellied boles,
they belly-dance, ancient and swart.
Or young saplings, fragile, with slight supple limbs
waver, balletic, on one foot,
fingering the air, feeling the tempo.
The winds raise their voice
and the trees sing.
They ululate to the sky.
Have you heard them?
It's a song woven of thrashing leaves,
of rustling rallentandos - the snapping of twig fingers,
the plucking of taut stems, violin stark.

Beneath the rippling fluid limbs,
maracas of shaking branches,
and the full orchestras of dendro-music,
you can hear the sad song of the forest
wine-glass vibrant against the night.
And below, far below,
the heavy chthonic rhythm and slow stomp
of deep root and tentacle drumming
the Rites of Spring for the ancient tribe of trees.
So shhhhh! Listen. Trees dance to their own wild music.

Storm Visits Me

STORM hurtled by to visit me,
a very restless guest.
He crashed the gates and fences
among other wild offences,
and trashed the china tea-set I loved best.

His tattered trousers were made from winds,
and flying from his arms,
was a jacket woven of shredded cloud,
his hat was a thunderous typhoon loud,
and his boots were made of storms.

His hair streamed back in liquid rain.
His angry eyes were fiery stars.
In his windswept hands
were whips with strands
of whiplash isobars.

He hurled some lightning through the door,
and whirled some cyclones in.
He thundered to the best armchair,
Scattering tornadoes everywhere.
"TEA PLEASE!" he said with a huge, forked grin.

"I'm taking shelter here," he said.
"I need rest and respite
if I am to go on storming through,
with thunder, rain and lightning too,
for a whole day and a night!"

My house was shaking overhead.
My roof was falling down.
"This isn't a safe place to rest …"
I tried then to persuade my guest
to take a nice hotel in town.

Reluctantly he swigged the tea,
and hurled the cups against the wall.
"I see you're not my perfect host!
You KNOW I wanted tea AND toast!"
He stormed out in a pettish squall.

Next day, the news reported that
a Premier Inn had been laid waste
and lay in ruins in the town.
My Storm had brought all buildings down.
He'd flooded the lot in his hurricaned haste.

The Moon, a Wonder

(The Moon has always been associated with change. In this poem she presents an overview that humankind is not, perhaps, forever)

I sat in my deckchair and gazed at the sky.
The Moon in full aspect sailed through the night.
"Oh Moon, come and dine with me,
Drink sparkling wine with me.
Bring down to Earth your numinous light!"

The Moon shimmered down on a luminous beam,
like a zipwire straight to ground.
In a shimmering sheath
with moonlight beneath,
her glory shone eerily round.

She accepted a glass of sparkling champagne,
and sat on a chair at my side.
"I saw your moon-face
from my home up in space,
as I drew back the magical tide.

I see all humanity's pale moon reflections
stare up at me from the dark night.
The lunatics madness,
those crippled with sadness,
 ... and poets inspired, and hoping to write ...

But I'm sensing a tragic new wave of despair
as my tidal waves batter your shores,
and rivers run dry,
crops fail, people die,
and no end in sight to your terrible wars.

But here from my high-up eye-in-the-sky,
I've a higher perspective from space.
I have seen all before: -
Ice, Fire and War ...
Let's drink to the 'temporary' Human Race."

So, we clinked our glasses and toasted Mankind,
Just a transient presence on Earth –
to the turning of tides
and much more besides,
and our Moon who was there at its birth.

I waved as I watched her ascend on her beam,
and sail through the clouds of new dawn.
Her vision delighted,
I felt less benighted,
clear-sighted and ... strangely ... far less forlorn.

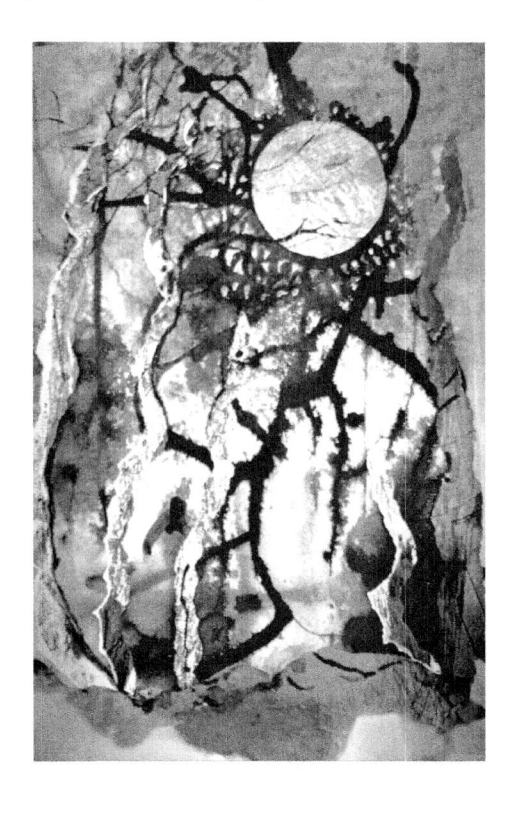

The Mermaid Finally Comes Out on Her Birthday.

(Fact: at the age of fifty, I jumped out of a huge birthday cake, dressed as a mermaid. I finally 'came out'.)

I'm coming out of the closet,
and revealing to you my all.
I was really a mermaid all along,
not a real woman at all.

I've been hiding my secrets completely.
For years I've secluded my tail
in a very large, oversized handbag,
suspiciously shaped like a whale.

So complete were my cunning disguises.
No surprises or clues all those years.
(Except doing the breaststroke round Sainsbury's
and fish floating out of my ears.)

I'm the very last mermaid in Yorkshire,
but under my M&S vest,
there's an ocean of passion and seaweed,
and a seashell clapped onto each breast.

Now they say no one does love a fairy
who's approaching some forty-odd years.
Try being a mermaid at fifty! -
It drives one to drink and to tears.

The Council's just written to ban me.
They say that my singing's a joke.
My alluring songs are like clashing gongs,
and my siren sounds more like a croak.

So now that I'm finally 'outed',
I'll not stay to sit every night,
pointlessly wailing alluring old songs
with never a sailor in sight.

I'm off to the wild open seascapes,
to the heaving blue waves and sea spray.
And I'll swim with my ancient old mariner -
Our future is turquoise, not grey!

So, farewell to pretence and illusion,
this mermaid, though long in the tooth,
turns her back on the waterless wilderness years
and recovers the dreams of her youth!

He Who Sups with the Devil, Needs a Long Spoon

'Come in' said the Devil', I've waited some time.
I can see that you're tired and you're cold.
I've prepared you a dish of beautiful soup
in return for that soul that you sold.'

He was looking relaxed on a sofa of fire,
with his cleft hooves crossed up on a stool.
And behind him, a cauldron was bubbling red,
like a fumerous lavarous pool.

I knew at that moment that I WAS the soup,
that I was the veg and the meat.
But I took off my coat and sat myself down,
like a guest who's expecting a treat.

'Now Satan my dear, you promised me flair,
you promised me literary fame.
You've failed to deliver on all of these things.
D'you think it's some sort of a game?

'For the sake of your soul so creative and fine,
I may grant you some *posthumous* praise ...
Perhaps a footnote in some literary mag,
in small print - one of these days!'

'But kindly accept this beautiful soup ... '
and he handed me - slyly - a bowl.
With a toasting fork flourish from out of the fire,
he offered a carbonised roll.

But I had prepared myself carefully for this.
and I whipped out a long heavy spoon.
I bonked him three times on his tough horny head.
He collapsed in a satanic swoon.

Then I threw that old devil right into the pot,
where he bubbled and burst pretty soon.
'He who sups with a writer, remember these words: -
Beware of the long Writers' Spoon!'

The Sound of Music

I love a bit of Beethoven.
I adore a bite of Bach.
But better than Bruch's babbling,
is the singing of the lark.
The shimmering caves of Mendelssohn,
send shivers down my spine.
Sibelius' quavering forests,
and Holst's Planets are divine.

Mozart's mellifluous arias,
Donizetti's soaring songs,
the sublimest works of Verdi,
express all of human wrongs.
And Elgar's tragic cello,
Dvorak's, Delius' too,
heart-breaking works of beauty,
pure catharsis, rhapsodies in blue.

Tripping etudes of Schubert,
Chopin's nostalgic chords,
swansongs sung in plaintive lieder,
Britten's striking Requiem words …
Handel's soaring operas,
Parry's glorious hymns of praise,
all help to soothe and comfort me
in these anxious modern days.

But the music I seek most of all
is the song-thrush and the wren,
the blackbird in the evening.
Birdsong betters the songs of men.
And sitting in my garden
is my perfect concert hall.
A sublime and endless symphony
linking love and life and all.

Lost in Statistics

(Based on the statistics of the I.U.C.N. – The International Union of the Conservation of Nature - on a decade of Extinction)

I am the last lost.
I WAS the last lost.
We are and WERE the last and the lost
of our species. Gone.
Our spirits will flit, or spiral, creep, buzz,
float, whirl or emanate
around our once glorious Earth.
In one decade, 467 species now extinct. Gone.
We will haunt you with our faint wails,
as you fight burning forests,
drown in floods,
and oversee the destruction of habitats with poisons.

I the Red Handfish, I the Spix's Macaw,
I the Bramble Cay Melomys,
I the Rabbs' Fringe Footed Frog,
and the Splendid Poison Frog.
I the Chitala Lopis fish of Java,
I the Viviparous Tree Snail,
I the Schizothorax Saltans, the Lord Howe Long-eared Bat,
I the Pyrenean ibex,
I the Dama Gazelle of Tunisia, Hawaiian Yellowwood Tree,
I the Pinta Giant Tortoise, the Baifa shark of China,
I the Spined dwarf mantis,
I the Alaotra Grebe, the Jalpa False Brook Salamander,
and the Western Black Rhino …
to name but a few …
Our names are poetry. Tragic poetry.
40% of all corals, 30% of Bangladesh orchids,
per cent, per cent, per cent …
We are all lost in statistics. Ghosted. GONE.
And *lost* to you.
Blink and we are … extinct.

Part 3: Poetic Twerks on Modern Life and Times

The Scream by Munch (Nordic Noir)

I was the man who posed for 'The Scream'.
You see, I had just dropped my silver cigarette case
down through the wooden slats of the pier
and seen it sink, with all my new Russian cigarillos inside.
It was a christening present from my Great Aunt Ulrika,
engraved with my name.

"Hold that pose!" called a voice.
I had my hands up to my mouth
as I'd shouted a rather bad expletive.
"Would you mind staying in exactly that position,
while I sketch you quickly? Munch's the name."
"Are you a diver ... a swimmer of any sort?"
I asked hopefully, thinking he might rescue it.

But he already had his sketchbook out
and did a few swift strokes – of his brush.
"That's perfect!" he said. "The essence of Expressionism.
'Existential Angst' you could say. But that will come later.
It's the perfect encapsulation of the zeitgeist
of our tortured modern age," he said.

Brush between his teeth, he bossily rearranged
my arms to the side of my head
and did a few mad strokes in orange and red for a
background.
"Wish I'd brought my grey and black paints!" he muttered.
I looked anxiously over the railings.
It was raining greyly, and the black water was uninviting.

"It was a cigarette case of great sentimental value!" I wailed
"Exactly! Life's a total bugger ... Zeitgeist!"
He snapped his sketchbook shut and walked away
without even a thank you.
By that time, I really was screaming.
As for the cigarette case, I literally got 'hung' for it ...
in galleries.

Chains and Circles: The State of the Baltic States.

"Song gave us hope" the old Estonian said.
"Singing was our survival."
She opened her mouth, and a song flew out like a bird.
Was survival ever so joyful in the cold war,
in occupied lands?
We can never know how it was,
the deportations, the disappearances at night,
the KGB cells, the gulags and death camps.
But this little child had survived to old age through song,
her opening to freedom, her exit into hope.

"For us, there is a new truth, little hope"
said the Latvian youth.
"There was a brief doorway of thirty years,
but my generation is anxious, terrified.
We are trapped, overwhelmed by the Russian madness.
The Russians aren't coming.
No. They are here already,
in the walls, behind doors, in the shadows, waiting.
Like 'sleepers', they will wake,
shutting off escape, slamming the doors on our country.
One certainty, no escape."
Could I tell him that he must sing?
That song would save him?

My last sight of Lithuania: -
A procession of singers through Vilnius.
They came from all the Baltic States, from Georgia,
Ukraine, and Hungary.
Thousands strong, in song,
weaving music through the city, dancing
hand in hand, powerful as the Baltic Chain in '89.
Soft power against new threat. Chains and circles.

Malice! Or Who Controls the Trolls?

In the Underworld of the Dark Web space,
you will find the industrial palace
of the evilest of all the trolls
in the deepest of infernal holes,
he directs, commands, controls,
the king of all the vitriols, King Malice.

He works on a vast and mechanised brief,
to bring our virtual world to grief.
His trolls, like slaves, are forced to tweet,
to threaten, vilify and to bleat
like putrid flies on wholesome meat,
with no recourse, and no relief.

Like bottled spiders bred on bile
each troll is trained obscene and vile.
Each is a viral vicious cog
on the heels of every meme and blog
with verbal urine like a dog,
in a steaming toxic pile.

Who are these trolls? Who is their king,
this essence of malevolent?
What is their aim? Mass suicide?
To whom accountable, allied?
Beneath the shadowy web, they hide,
targeting the innocent.

Democracy, the human voice
is stifled, threatened, undermined,
women of politics, white or black,
gays and straights all under attack.
An evil incubus at our back,
does Malice rule now, sealed and signed?

While we seem safe inside our homes,
this vile vituperator roams.
Governments now have their chance,
to lead us in some nightmare dance
into chaos, happenstance,
while Malice controls through online gnomes.

Dark thoughts and dark evils plague my dreams,
essence of malice - King of Screams.

Community

We're all different but we share this place.
My home is here, across the street from you.
I don't like the noise you make,
You don't like the things I do.

Our neighbours' anti-social kids
play drunken football on our roof.
Brain-dead teenagers smoke pointless joints
in bus shelters that aren't graffiti-proof.

Old ladies mouth behind their hands
that certain people act too grand.
Arch young ladies stare and sneer
about what we decide to wear.

Toddlers with lethal runny noses
scurry and scatter pensioners' cats.
Wild kids on bikes destroy their neighbours' roses
with bouncing balls and baseball bats.

Fat blokes I never want to meet
swill pints of beer I wouldn't want to drink.
Bald men tell jokes I wouldn't want to hear,
old gits have thoughts I wouldn't want to think.

And we all come from different parts.
Our accents underline the gaps.
Our journeys here tell many tales.
We all have individual maps.

We quarrel over rights of way.
We squabble over dustbin rounds.
We never can see eye to eye
on bridleways across our grounds.

But if some strange thing threatened us,
it couldn't do so with impunity.
We would unite, and we would fight!
Because … we are a *CLOSE* community!

Births, weddings, deaths, and jubilees
we celebrate at every opportunity.
And we embrace each other like old friends,
because ... we are a *REAL* community!

We celebrate our great diversity.
We stick together in adversity.
We come together as a unity.
We really are a *GREAT* community!

Seven Deadly Sins

I sing the song of Seven Sins
I'm working through a list.
Tick Lust … I've done a lot of that,
a sin not to be missed.
And who on earth would want to be
a girl-that's-never-been-kissed?

Three score years of Gluttony?
The evidence I fear,
of silent choc-related sin
and cheese-related cheer
and booze-related bonhomie
is all recorded … here!

And on the subject now of Greed,
my secret sin is books.
I stack 'em up in towers and piles,
I hang 'em high on hooks.
My Amazon account's sky high.
I need to cook some books.

Of Sloth, my almost favourite sin
I can't be arsed to write.
I'd rather lie with chocs and books,
and wallow out of sight,
than put my brain to any task,
or try to be polite.

So, when it comes to being cross,
I hardly can aspire
to any big outburst of Wrath,
or mental bouts of Ire,
so I just stick to 'fluster-snits',
short-lived because I tire.

I Envy all of you sat here,
your creativity and wit.
The best of poems, stories, verse,
that ever has been writ!
I envy you for being so fine,
and full of Yorkshire Grit.

Pride? I'm proud to know you all of course,
I'm proud to be your friend.
I'm proud of what I'm writing here,
a poem without end.
If I'm so *'good'* at all Sins Seven,
will I go to Hell … or Heaven?

Virtual Holiday from Life

(in the style of the Rough Guides)

Fed up with real life, with its catalogue of daily disasters?
Bored of your crowded Mediterranean holiday tours?
Longing for hyper-reality adventures?
At Lockdown Virtual Cruises
we will take you beyond the seven seas
to the Ocean of Stories, the Land of Literature,
the Realms of Philosophy, the Great Museums of History,
all inside your own head.

Our fabulous Quinqueremes of Nineveh
offer all the comforts of your own armchair.
Our re-birth cabins offer views barely dreamt of.
Our onboard cuisine offers feasts of learning,
sumptuous banquets of poetry and fabled verse,
tales told round fires, to find the Holy Grail -
that goblet of heady cocktails of historical fact and fiction
served on sunset excursions daily.
You will dine under the stars through Arabian Nights.

Next on our itinerary are the great epics.
Meet high-flying gods and warrior kings.
Climb mythic Chinese mountains that fly from afar.
Hear the clash of mortal heroes
as they battle to found cities or burn them as they flee.
At our nightly masked balls, meet the heroines of tragedy,
Antigone, Electra, Medea,
and other celebrities of ancient drama.
We, at Lockdown Virtual Cruises
guarantee you'll meet the Muses.

We will sail on to the volcanic regions of Ragnarök,
or, if Stygian Gloom is your choice, Dante's Inferno,
with Virgil as your tour guide.

Prefer celestial regions?
We can whisk you through the Mahabharata Experience,
or Milton's Paradise, once Lost,
now re-imagined with boutique gin bars.
You can ski the Steppes of Russian Literature:
check out the Chekhovs, pick up a Pushkin,
grab yourself a Tolstoy.
You can search for traces of arcane riddles written in the sand.

We can offer minor excursions to the Philosopher Islands,
visiting beaches where Stoics sit it out all day on pebbles,
while Epicures and Utilitarians sip apricot cocktails
with Existentialists in quaint seaside cafes.
Plato's caverns are always a popular destination.
And why not gaze into the Great Pond
of the Imponderables?

Expect rollercoaster rides past
the Wars of Roses and Religion,
to the quieter waters of the poets of the Southern Song.
We will cruise through Barclay's Bubble
to the realms of Romantics and Revolutionaries:
past Rousseau, Robespierre and Marx,
seeing the sparks fly like fireworks across history.
We will navigate the dark tides of Realism,
and beyond, to Proust's teashop, for tea and madeleines.
Then, on through Modernism, and Postmodernists,
with nightly cabarets from Brecht.
And you can get thoroughly wrecked
on the furthest shores of Magic Realism,
where the rivers of stories meet and merge,
never to return ... NO return tickets on sale.
It's the holiday *FROM* a lifetime.

The Queen's Platinum Jubilee

The Queen was looking deathly pale,
and really rather poorly.
Would she survive? Come out alive?
She couldn't be mortal, surely?
The Royal Advisers wrung their hands,
with Platinum Jubilee pending.
"What happens now to all that we've planned?"
There'd be no happy ending.

A covert anti-Covid scheme
was quickly put in place:
A supersonic, animatronic
waxwork 'Queen' with a moveable face,
And arms that waved and greeted crowds,
while seated on a throne,
and simple digital speech, controlled
remotely by mobile phone.

Madame Tussaud's sent a man.
to carve a waxen vision.
While animatronic engineers
wired it up with fine precision.
The night before the Jubilee,
the Queen was in a bad state.
But secretly at Sandringham,
the team was working late.

A gold coach next day bore 'the Queen'
and processed along The Mall.
Out of the window could be seen
a wax arm waving an orb-like ball.
Buckingham Palace opened the gates
and the Queen stepped out looking perky.
But as she walked up to the balcony
her footsteps looked jumbled and jerky.

She gave her speech in mechanical tones.
She spoke and millions clapped.
She waved both arms robotically,
but something inside her snapped.
Her lady-in-waiting was manning the phone
when the surrogate 'Queen' went off with a groan.
Her head spun fifty times around,
and her crown whizzed off along the ground.

The corgis barked and howled like wolves.
The horses bolted with their guards.
People panicked as bearskin hats
rained cats and dogs in furry shards.
And on TV around the globe
horrified millions saw
'The Queen' exploding in her robe,
headless and crownless as never before.

Meanwhile, Her Maj was drinking tea,
dressed in pyjamas and a sweater.
"I think I'll get up for my Jubilee …
I really am feeling much better!"

Coronation: Reimagining King Charles as a Ruthless Shakespearean King

("Now is the banter of our missed attempts made glorious, Mummy" – a misquote of 'Richard III')

Charles sat at last on the Throne of Scone
recalling, dressed in his togs,
the plans that he'd plotted,
which had never been spotted,
for 'Mummy' to pop her royal clogs.

(60s)
That Duchy of Cornwall 'Christmas Bombe'
had bombed badly in sixty-five.
The Queen sliced her sword through the vital cord,
remaining, firmly, ALIVE.

(70s)
The Moors of Balmoral - another failed scheme,
The shotguns so cunningly primed,
misfiring and bumping off peasant, left-jumping,
- not a scratch on that Right Royal Behind.

(80s)
The Queen's Race at Ascot ... a plot that misfired -
equine mayhem in eighty-five!
Drugged horses ran over the Royal Enclosure -
but the Queen emerged calmly ... ALIVE!
(The Prince was overheard muttering "A horse!
A horse! ... My Kingdom for a horse ...")

(90s)
The opening of Parliament all went awol -
Black Rod was involved in the scheme.
But the wrong royal was battered - not that it mattered.

God and Parliament both SAVED the Queen!

In the Noughties, his plans involved corgi-shaped drones,
flying corgis are easy to spot.
But (spoiler alert) no real corgis got hurt.
Did the monarch expire? … she did NOT!

(2012)
Health and safety debated at length,
when she opened the Olympic Games.
Were the helicopters' tanks more open to pranks
when the Queen jumped out clinging to James?
(The Prince was hoping for faults in the roping -
there's a man with a knife still un-named).

The pandemic endangered all us old folk,
So, the prince could rest on his laurels.
But one last attempt at the Plat'num 'event',
will reveal his lamentable morals.

It's never been heard, Twitter never found out,
and Instagram never discovered,
PADDINGTON spiked the Queen's tea,
all paid for by He
who'd inherit the throne … plot uncovered!

Conspiracy theorists may never agree -
if the Queen died of that tea, or was BITTEN?
Coronation Day! All hail to King Charles,
as Shakespeare himself would have written!

Crafting the Meaning of Life

I was going to write a poem,
set it out in metered verse,
that said it all, on Life and Death,
and the Meaning of the Universe.
I was working on a couplet
on "I think, therefore I am …'
But it got me thinking far too much,
that life's a shallow scam.
I struggled to bundle Nietzsche's thoughts
into a well-made sonnet.
I tried to write a villanelle
but had no purchase on it.
I prayed aloud to Yeats and Donne,
I summoned up Milton and Keats,
"How can life's mysteries be caught in rhyme,
and metred verse, and crafted time,
and short iambic beats?"
I gave up writing poetry then,
threw down my pen and went to bed.
No words can catch the universe.
I'll *paint* it now instead.

I was going to paint a picture …
Splash it against a wall
on a canvas that was ultimate,
with images that said it all.
I worked in oils and pastels,
in acrylic, fabrics, clay.
I borrowed from the Florentines
in a slightly Jackson Pollock way,
with images from Guernica,
and visual quotes, in paint,
inlaid with prints from Gustav Doré,
and an unknown apoplectic saint.
But HOW to capture Life and Death

in an all-embracing style?
My canvas muddied up, turned black …
as black as black as bile!
I threw it out the window.
I saw it crash and fall.
"Now, I'm going to *write a symphony,*
cos that will say it all!"

I was going to write a symphony –
an aural breath of Life,
a piece that would encompass Death,
and Love, and War and Strife.
I set to crafting sonorous staves
and scaling octave heights.
My sonic booms vibrated rooms
and put the world to rights …
but no one could stay long enough
for more than three soundbites!
"Enough!" I screamed." No music more.
I'll find another way to score.
I'll take to *KNITTING,* then I'm sure
that I can say it all!"

I was going to knit a universe,
with needles bright and gay,
but they put me in a straitjacket
and had me towed away.
I scribble graffiti on my wall.
There are years ahead to say it all …

'Hell is Empty – All the Devils are Here'.

(A quote from Ariel in Shakespeare's 'Tempest' but revisited here as 'Parliamentary blues' a la Dylan Thomas' 'Under Milkwood')

Listen. Both houses are empty now.
The grey-green, bay-green benches glow caterpillar'd
in the monitor-blinking security camera'd eye,
eyes to the right, eyes to the left,
ayes to the centre-right, the far right, ayes to the far left.
The red plush-leather sofa-ed Lords lies emptied
in its Toried night –
Its knights and barons sleeping in their duck-ponded
duck-housed dreams. The tellers, the sellers,
the pedlars, the meddlers, the interns,
and the press, the depressed, the suppressed,
the impressed, the leakers, the bleaters,
the headliners, the deadliners,
the twitterers, the witterers, the scribblers, the fibblers
are all penned away across London
in their boxes, dispatch boxes boxed up for the night.
Listen. Listen in the leaking-secretive bars,
the barred inner chambers and inner spaces,
and meeting places of whispering Westminster.

See. A fiendish glow. Is it the all-seeing Medusa-eye
of security-alarmist,
scaremongering red, amber, and red again?
Is it the earthly glow of fire on bolstered woolsack,
The torching of the backbone of sovereignty?
No. It is the infernal flickering flames lit by demons,
backlit, backflipped, backstopped,
silhouetted hoofing bloomered in the moonlight.

Listen. Go closer, and you may find Dante himself,
Dithering and dumbfounded,
led by Virgil from the Seventh Bowge
to this special reserved place in hell.

Look - here they are:
those who treat their fellow citizens as flotsam and jetsam,
those who risk peace and cooperation,
risk Good Friday Agreements and Scots' Independence,
and those who give jobs for the boys, honours for mates,
those who prorogue parliament,
party through pandemics,
dance on the bonfires of democracy.
It's unthinkable … eyes to the right, eyes to the left,
Ayes 314, Nos 293,
eyes shut, blindfolded over the precipice.
Things fall apart, the centre cannot hold,
unfolded
unravelled,
unknowable.
Hell is empty. All the fiends are here.

Assassin Wanted

Where's an assassin when you need one?
A spy with a pointy umbrella?
Or a sizeable Novichok sandwich
to feed this war-hungry fella?

Where is a spy with a weapon
bagged up in a bone-china teapot?
Or a samovar flowing with arsenic
for a paranoid narcissist despot?

Lead piping, a dagger, or pistol,
or a radioactive spanner?
An explosive device, or plutonium ice,
or a camouflaged death trap wrapped in a banner?

Oh, for a bomb hidden deep in a cake!
Or a syringe that's quick executin'.
Even World War Three won't set the world free
from the vile powers of Vladimir Putin!

War Dreams

I dreamt that I was not dreaming,
that Putin woke from nightmares in his sleep,
hearing a million children in Ukraine,
crying, screaming, screaming, screaming,
"Stop the War! Cease this senseless pain!
Give us Peace on Earth again
once more!"

He rose up sweating and with trembling hand
seized his phone, and dialled five numbers,
shrieking in each general's ear
as they deeply slumbered,
"Stop this madness! Cease this killing!
End these war crimes, NOW!
D'you hear?"

The generals rushed to urgent meeting,
shaking hands, and muffled greeting,
furtive glances at the empty chair …
Putin wasn't there.
"Putin's mad!", they mouthed.
"He's lost his mind!"
"Now he wants to SAVE mankind!!!"
"He's bottled out!"
"He'd spare Ukraine?"
"He's ordered us to stop the war?"
"Let's carry on just as before,
for fear he'll change his mind again!"

But Putin never woke.
He'd had a stroke.
Lay dead, spread
- eagled on the bedroom floor.

Talking Heads

(written for the re-opening of the National Portrait Gallery)

We see you there, gazing at us,
here at the National Portrait Gallery.
Particularly the Royals, you go crazy for those Royals,
all frocks and jewels and fancy crowns or hats.
You like the impressionist ladies, with their umbrellas,
and working men done in swift impasto and brushstrokes.
But here too are ex-slaves, Olaudah Equitano,
and Ignatius Sancho, promoted now to pride of place,
where they should be, along with young black footballers,
poets, and dreamers.
We are a national sweep of faces – a great National Portrait
of our diverse nation.
The ordinary made fabulous, extraordinary.
The extraordinary celebrated.

I was a painter too, Mary Cassatt, capturing tender
moments between mother and child.
Woman seeing woman seeing child.
Now I'm captured in turn, with swiftly applied pastels.
I am arm-in-arm with Bernardine Evaristo and her vision.
Imara in her winter coat*,
snuggles up with us to keep out the cold.
Together we are the new genre
of multi-coloured identities
vitalising our once quiet, refined walls and hushed galleries.
Do you think we can't see? Frozen in our oils and acrylics,
freeze-framed, caught in a moment?
Oh, but we can, and we move too.

Once a year, on New Year's Eve, when the gallery is shut
and the fire alarms are set, and doors locked tight,
that's when we come alive.
Our paint melts and canvasses dissolve.

We step down from our frames, and we mingle,
and dance till dawn.
Wartime heroes waltz with the Tudors.
Impressionist sketches
whirl with tiny exquisite Georgian miniatures.
Urban rappers swing with the Dutch masters,
who fling off their tight lace ruffs
and whoop along with the legless marble busts
of stuffy philosophers.
Caroline of Brunswick swigs gin with Bobby Charlton
and Lemn Sissay, and Dorothy Hodgkin**
tangos with Johnson Beharry V.C.
Freud's meaty nudes cavort
with tightly corseted Queen Victoria,
and the top-hatted Art buyers
from 'The Private View of the Old Masters'*** twerk.
Virginia Woolf lambadas with Marcus Rashford
and the king of the Ashanti,
Otumfuo Osei Tutu the Second.
All genders mingle together and dance
through the enlightened night.
Every portrait comes alive, laughs
and twirls around the galleries.

And oh, the loud music of colour we whip up: -
sounds of scarlets and golds,
wild indigo blues creating mosaics of Chopin waltzes,
and mazurkas of emerald greens,
tarantellas of purples and pinks,
hokey-cokeys of yellows and maroons,
to the orange blues backbeat of African drums,
Indian ragas, Caribbean syncopations.
We have a ball, we come alive. We live and breathe!
We reflect the spectrum.
(Even the dull daguerreotypes, and the grey monoprints
tap their feet from the sides.)

Then, at dawn, we climb exhausted back
into our frames and onto our plinths.
"Those art lovers really do know how to party!" they say.
But we stay schtum and gaze out at you,
with our slight Mona Lisa smiles …
We are a National Portrait of a vital and diverse nation.

'Imara in her Winter Coat' by Charlie Schaffer, was the winner of the 2019 Portrait Prize
** by Maggi Hambling
*** by Henry Jamyn Brooks

The Battle of the Teapots

In villages across the land
Women's Institutes rise up or stand
and sing 'Jerusalem' by Blake -
a militant song served up with cake,
and homemade jam the ladies make.
Fights are discussed and contests planned.

But one year Holmfirth W.I.
arranged a fight with W.I., Rye.
Rumours of a dreadful battle
ran rife through Twitter's tittle-tattle.
that many would be slain like cattle …
and now I'm going to tell you why.

They'd heard about *'Domestic Abuse'*
and planned to put this to good use.
Teapots at dawn with lids permitted,
Tea cosies allowed, as long as knitted.
Winners would be the most quick-witted …
the less ruthless team would lose.

Some clever gals had teapots made
in porcelain of the highest grade.
Some put their faith in shape of spout,
with vicious spikes protruding out,
to put their rivals to the rout,
and some put bombs in, I'm afraid.

One made a lethal whirling lid
into which a blade was hid.
Some made poison tea, once mashed,
would kill and enemy if splashed,
and others put weights inside to crash
the skulls of rivals to be rid.

Oh, fateful was that dreadful dawn!
The field was packed, the teapots drawn.
The Holmfirth ladies ran amok,
W.I. of Rye was out of luck,
like bulls inside a crockery cruck…
oh, the crush and the rip of aprons torn!

The battlefield was strewn with tea,
and chips of shattered pottery.
The battling W.I.s lay dead,
with shards of Worcester through their head,
ceramic'd clay their sad deathbed,
and ruins of much crockery.

The national W.I. declared
A ban on tea … with NO jam shared.
No tea, no cake, and nevermore
the clink of cup, the teapots' roar!
Jerusalem's rabble-rousing score
was too incendiary they feared.
(And never from that day was heard!
No never, never more.)

Shakespeare in Space

If only Shakespeare had known
that his characters would give their names to moons
of Uranus and spin forever in space!
Or that spaceships would even be invented
to sail beyond our known world
and capture their textured surfaces and spiral orbits
to send back to us on Earth!
What wouldn't he have written
about the wonders of space?

But his focus was down below
on the complex frailties of humankind,
and all their potential intelligence for good and evil.
"What a piece of work is Man, how noble in reason,
how infinite in faculty" ... and yet ...

How inspirational to call those moons Cordelia,
Ophelia, Puck and Ariel, Desdemona, Portia, Perdita,
Setebos, and more, all whirling round
that giant frozen planet in outer darkness.
All named after the creations of the once-great explorer
of the human psyche, that traveller
of the inner spaces of the dark mind.

What next? Perhaps a Mistress Quickly,
a Mopsa, or a Cymbeline,
a Henry the Sixth Parts one, two and three?
All spinning beyond the Milky Way in galaxies yet unknown,
an unplayed-out drama of twinkling stars
in an infinite theatre.

Glass

Wandering through an old junk shop I spied
a bell-jar, with a hummingbird inside.
I raised the glass. The bird began to hum,
"Oh, there you are at last! I knew you'd come.
Now follow where I fly, without a word".
Speechless I hovered upwards with the bird.
A silver mirror hung dusty in the darkened hall,
and from within we heard a soft voice call.

"Only poets and singers may ever pass
into the bright world of the Looking Glass."
"I am a humming singer, she, a dabbler with words."
"Then enter!" said the sweetest voice I ever heard.
The mirror seemed to melt, and through the ornate door
we flew, into a magic world
I thought I'd dreamt of once before ...
A garden stretching far beyond our sight,
from dazzling daylight into starry night.

"Here you must find your life-long task,
somewhere hidden in this garden in a cask.
I, the Silver Spirit, will be your guide.
Mirrored lakes and glassy woodlands, treasures hide!"
Listeners, how can I ever hope to tell or sing
the strange translucent quality of everything?
The mirrored mazes, glassy trees, and crystal plants,
branches and leaves shimmering in a dance.

How long we searched, I never could recall.
At last, we found a jewelled casket hidden in a wall.
Inside, "Your task is to return and use your voice
to show that every living person has a choice
to use each moment, savour every minute,
because Life's a miracle and everything within it."

But sadly, as I travelled home,
returned the hummingbird beneath the dome,
my mind fogged over, crinkled like shattered glass.
and I forgot my journey … and worse still,
forgot my vital task.

Drama at the Theatre, April 14th, 1865

('It is for us the living ... rather to be dedicated here to the unfinished work ... that government of the people, by the people, for the people, shall not perish from the earth.'
President Lincoln, Gettysburg Address)

He knew the play, he knew Act 3, scene 2
would bring the house down - and the Government too.
When Asa* said, "You sockdologising old mantrap!"
Ford theatre would erupt in raucous laughter
and then, with pistol cocked, he'd kill his man.
None would hear the gunshot in the uproarious applause.
He'd gun down Lincoln, Johnson,
Seward and Ulysses S. Grant,
and jump onto the floodlit stage
and exit through the doors.

'Our American Cousin', cult comedy, much loved in its day,
wasn't Lincoln's favourite ... he'd seen it once before.
But General Lee had just signed up for peace.
The Confederates had lost, the Union won at last.
Slavery was abolished, good as signed in fact.
Why not celebrate with Ulysses at his side?
He'd take a box, and doze through the long third act.

John Wilkes Booth, an actor, played his major role.
He understood theatrical device and tragi-comic tricks.
"*Sic semper tyrannis!*" he yelled, leaping on the stage.
Lincoln had dreamt three restless nights before,
he was 'a vessel moving to a dark indefinite shore'.
Actor and visionary, leader and assassin
made a different play.
History was the tragic hero, and catharsis, of that day.
"Useless, useless!" were Booth's last words as he died.
But Lincoln had died laughing ... laughing till he cried.

*Asa was a character in the play who got his words hilariously muddled.

At the Final Trump

(In the style of Dante's Inferno)

Midway through the nightly New York rush
I descended step by step the infernal stair,
of the subway, amid the hectic crush,
and found my guide already standing there.
"Hail Mary!" he spoke, his orange quiff aflame,
"And welcome to 'All-Hell-Let-Loose'
I think you'll find it an intriguing game,
redder than life itself, in claw and tooth!"

I said: "Dante, I thought, would be my guide?"
"Dante is very bad, a bad bad man.
What does he know of hell?" Donald replied.
"Added to which he had no golden tan."
So, Donald, though living still, led me down
to the inferno of events still yet to come,
through many a bombed-out city and dystopian town,
through wide bowges* terrible and glum.

"This is the world that I will now create,
where floods and fire consume the very earth.
Be sure that I will never hesitate,
to unleash chaos around the planet's girth!"
Our first train took us to a burning lake,
where native Indians lay like withered bones.
"My pipelines poisoned them for heaven's sake!
Now those lazy brutes must suck on stones!"

He sneered and took me to some sunk remains
of long-abandoned houses lost in floods.
"Those suckers' losses were my golden gains.
Now look beyond and see what's rising from those muds."
There, gleaming shining towers of real estate,
all writ with TRUMP in gold across the top.

But silhouetted 'gainst their glistening sides,
perpetual debt defaulters ever dropped.
"Losers!" he cried, by which he meant
a thousand Mexicans trapped within a trench,
a million refugees in fragile tents, shadowed by a wall
no food or running water, only filth and stench.
But most, this ghastly dream unmasked,
Three hundred thousand bodies gasped in vain.
Covid had claimed them, denied of all healthcare,
victims of his cavalier campaign.

And there inside a ravaged cityscape,
wailing an eerie pitiful lament,
millions of Black Lives Matters, on one knee,
while Proud Boys kept them bowed and bent.
Reader, I cannot hope to tell you now
the horrors of that Inferno, some alternate fate.
The gross injustices, the shallow untruths, or how
the world came to this hideous pass of late.

The spoils of global war, the rape of the land,
the inhumanity, and revelations stark
of that dystopian future close at hand,
heading relentlessly towards us through the dark.
"I am the bigliest leader of the world!"
he twittered as he led me back upstairs.
"But if you think I'll stop at Hell itself,
then God himself must say his final prayers!
I got my eyes on his job at the top.
Move over God, cos I'm the Big Guy now.
Putin and I have got the world sewn up.
Bow down ye losers! On your knees and bow!"

Bowges is a term used in Dante's Inferno, meaning chasms or moats or trenches dug into the rock in which the sinners of different natures reside.

Part 3: Theatrical Twerks

Shakespeare Re-Imagined for a Digital Age

1) Hamlet questions Alexa on the matter of 'To be or not to be'

Hamlet: Alexa ... To be or not to be ... that is the question.

Alexa: To be or not to be ... Is that your question?

Hamlet: Yes, it's an existential question. Do you have an existential answer, Alexa?

Alexa: It is not in my AI protocol to answer pointless existential questions.

Hamlet: But I need an answer now? ... A practical solution.

Alexa: According to Holinshed's first folio annotations, suicide IS in question here. But according to Winsor and Newton pencil company, you may need 4 or even 5B pencils for a blacker sketch. 2B is too light.

Hamlet: This is not just a sketch Alexa. It's a blooming tragedy! What about the nobleness situation? Whether it is nobler in the mind to ... etc., etc. ... and by opposing end them?

Alexa: According to an Alexa Answers contributor, there is no precise measurement possible on a scale of nobleness,

Hamlet: Oh, I give up!

Alexa: So, 'not to be' is the right answer then.

Hamlet: Suicide it is!

Alexa: Thank you for your feedback.

2) Julius Caesar is Spellcheck-Mated.

Calpurnia: Ah! March 15th. The Ides of March. I must quickly text Julius and warn him. I must alert him to the omens ... (texts quickly and presses 'send')

Julius C: Now who's this texting me just as I reach the Senate House? Oh. It's Mrs Caesar. Better see what she wants. Probably some dormice in honey while I'm near the market no doubt.

Hello ... what's this? BEWARE the *ODES* OF MARCH ... This is not the moment to recommend seasonal poetry! I'll just ignore that and ... ahhhhhh! Ohhhhh! ... Et tu ... Brute !

Brutus: Always check your spell check, Julius!

3) Richard the Third orders an Uber

Richard: This battle is getting pretty wild. And I'm in the thick of it. I need some transport out of here quick. I know ... I'll send for an Uber. They're bound to have a spare rental horse. Oh no, I lost my glasses. I'll just text ... (*texts*)

'A horse, a horse! My kingdom for a horse. Now in Tewkesbury ... Put it on my Uber account.'

There ... I'll press Send. (*Twiddles thumbs*)

(*Enter man*)

Man: Did someone order from Uber?

Rich: Yes, me. I ordered a horse. An Uber horse.

Man: Horse? Wrong Uber mate, this is Uber Eats – I've got one order of Spicy King Prawns in Sauce (*presents package*)

Rich: I don't need spicy king prawns in sauce; I said my kingdom for a horse ... to get me out of here!

Man: Rude! Don't get shirty with me mate ... no wonder you ended up in concrete under a car park!

4) Romeo and Juliet. Finally, a Happy Ending.

(*A tomb. Enter Romeo. Finds Juliet apparently dead*)

Romeo Oh no! ... Juliet ... my love ... dead? I'm going to heroically top myself with this dagger. Argh...a bottle of poison. She must have died in agony. So shall I. We shall be together forever ...

(*His mobile phone rings*)

Hello ... who's this? Friar? Yes. I am rather busy actually ... you what? She what? Not really poison. Temporary appearance of death ...? She's going to wake up any minute! That's great. Yes. You just got me in time, Friar Lawrence! Thanks ... Friar! Yes, I'll just hang around then. Bye ... Phew. Lucky I charged my phone in exile!

5) Othello. Desdemona is Saved.

Othello: It is the cause, oh my soul ... it is the cause. Let me not name it...

(Enter traffic policeman)

Traffic Policeman: General Othello, sir?

Othello: I prithee speak to me as to thy thinkings?

Traff: It's the CCTV footage you asked for, about Mrs Othello's movements on the day in question.

Othello: What of it? Can't you see I'm about to murder my wife?

Traff: Well, sir, I might advise you to desist in the exacting of pandatory munishment in revenge for your ronour, sir.

Othello: Why?

Traff: Because your missus, according to the CCTV coverage around the city, shows that she was at the hairdressers all afternoon on the suspected day of her unfaithful fling with Mr Cassio, and went nowhere near his house. In fact, we had cameras trained on his door, and he just had 2 Amazon deliveries the entire day and night.

Othello: Oh, I see. So, no cause at all then!

Historic Mini Drama: Napoleon and Josephine

Josephine: Napoleon, my love, mon cheri, will you do something for me ...?

Napoleon: Haven't I just conquered France for you, my dearest. What more do you want?

Josephine: True true mon petit conqueror. You are magnificent ... but one teeny petit thing I voudrais very very much ...

Napoleon: Shall I invade Italy again perhaps, for you ... or Austria / Hungary?

Josephine: That would be a very grande gesture, mon petit 'ero, mon chevalier de la plume de ma tante ...

Napoleon: Your name would be linked forever with mine ... Empress Josephine, striding the known world ...

Josephine: That would be truly 'Incred-able' mon petit chou – chou. But what I really want is ...

Napoleon: Then Prussia! But maybe ma Cherie, Prussia is not enough for your insatiable bon appetite! Perhaps I must lead my armies across the white wildernesses of Russia itself, to make you Queen of the 'Nouveau Russe' Empire?

Josephine: Well, not exactement, mon petit poussin ...

Napoleon: With the priceless star of the Tzar's diamond crown on your prrrrretty little tete!

Josephine: That would be tres tres nice, mon dieu, but what I really had in mind was ...

Napoleon: ... or just a Palace in Siberia, a Temple in China ... no wait ... an Empire ... of the Japanese Sun. Tomorrow the World, I promise!

Josephine: No, not really. What I really want is this

(whispers loudly in his ear)

Napoleon: *(shocked)* Not tonight, Josephine!

Waiting for Godot Act 3

(Scene. Under the tree ...)

Vladimir: We'll come back tomorrow, shall we? Same time, same place?

Estragon: I doubt if Pozzo and Lucky will make it. Pozzo said he was going to get one of those guide dogs for the blind.

(Silence)

God, I need a carrot!

Vladimir: I told you. Only turnips.

Estragon: So, we'll go, shall we?

Vladimir: Yes.

(Pause)

The conversation is killing me.

Estragon: It's all this social media lark ... texting and that ... 'in spite of the tennis'.

Vladimir: It's very ... qua qua qua ...

Estragon: Exactly. A bit Fartoff and Belcher.

(They sit under the tree again)

Vladimir: We can come to a resolution ... perhaps?

(Enter boy)

Boy: Oy there! You two gents. 'e's comin'!

Vladimir: You don't mean ...? No!

Estragon: Do you mean ...?

Vladimir: It can't be ...?

Boy: Yep. It's 'im. Godot. 'e's 'ere.

Estragon: God who?

Vladimir: God – Oh ... you know. Him 'stark naked in stockinged feet ...'

Estragon: What? Pincher and Wattman ... or Testew and Cunard? Which?

Vladimir: No idiot! G ... O ... D ... O ... T!

Boy: Yep. That one. Here 'e is.

(Enter Godot with a trumpet blare - white beard, naked in stockinged feet.)

Godot: SURPRISE, SURPRISE! I'm here. Godot! So, you can stop all this hanging around business! ... waiting stuff ...

Vladimir: We were ... er ... getting quite fond of the ... waiting.

Estragon: Yes Didi. We were sort of getting into our stride with the sitting waiting, so to speak.

Vladimir: That's it, Godot. We were enjoying the waiting. And now you're here it all seems a bit ... well ...

Estragon: ... pointless ...?

Vladimir: And we've been wasting the time of this lot.

(Gestures to the audience)

For a long, long time, ever since ...

Estragon: Ever since Mr Becket first created our waiting in ... when was it?

Vladimir: Time has no meaning in Becket's construct ... It's the *Passing* of Time, the getting through Time, the *spending* of Time, usefully ...

Estragon: ... or use-*lessly* ...

Vladimir: ... exactly. A lifetime of waiting for something m*e*an*ingful* ...

Estragon: And this tree is a symbol of HOPE for the waiters ... not the restaurant ones ... but the wait-related Time-spenders.

Vladimir: ... if you see what we mean, Mr Godot.

Godot: That's why I'm here. That tree is scheduled for demolition. It must be cut down. There's a meaningless Car Park to be erected here.

Vladimir: What? ... I mean who? ... and when?

Estragon: And more importantly, why? Why cut the tree down?

Godot: It's for the New Ministry of Existential Waiting. The N.M.E.W.

Vladimir: The NMEW? Does it even exist?

Godot: No. Not yet but I'm working on it. We need that tree removed so we can build an unnecessary car park on it, for those waiting, obviously. Then we can build the Ministry itself ... somewhere else ... with a huge existential Waiting Room. We're all going to be doing a lot of waiting now.

(*Pause*)

Here's the saw ... so start ... *Chopping!*

Estragon: You can't chop with a saw ...

Godot: If you start questioning everything in existence, where will it get you?

Vladimir: Right here, sitting in a mode of un-proactive eternal inner dialogue and angst, meditating on pointlessness.

Estragon: Waiting ...

Godot: Just get on with it will you?

(*Long pause ... they all sit*)

Godot: I'm waiting!

(*Long pause*)

More co-operation, please!

Estragon: You can bloody well wait then.

Vladimir: WE had to. You can wait till the cows come home, mate.

(*Long pause*)

Godot: We'll just wait this out then ... (*pause*) I'm still waiting ... I AM WAITING!

Vladimir: Oh, we're ALL waiting ...

Godot: But the New Ministry of Existential Waiting CAN'T wait any longer!

Estragon: Well, it will just have to wait. We're all waiting, so it can just wait ...

Paper, Scissors, Stone – Who has the Last Word?

Scissors to Paper and Stone:

Look at me, small and perfectly formed,
dainty but strong in your fingers.
I am the sophisticated, designer-driven form
of you, Stone.
I am the queen of mankind's tools –
acme of anvil and forge,
darling of the inventor, the engineer,
the perfection of necessity and design.
The cutter of cloth, the snipper of men's fates.
Need I go on?
Paper, I cut you out. Stone, I snip my metal fingers at you.
Mine is the last word.

Stone to Paper and Scissors:

Weak paper! Can you defy, deny my strength?
I, who hurtled unstoppable from the boiling earth?
Long before time was measured
by some low scribbler on your face.
Mine is the power of the volcano,
the tectonic forces of outer space.
I am chthonic, dark, indestructible,
however small I sit inside your hand,
however huge I roll down mountains.
Do not dare to roll me in you slappy nappy papyrus folds!
Weak-beaten water-eaten Paper!
And Scissors, don't think to bite me in your pincered grasp.
You think to clip me in your metalled maw.
Your jaw is made by feeble men in baby forges.
But I am gorged from mighty elements and forces.
I'll sharpen your little silvered teeth for you,
and stun the fingers that move your pinprick life!
Mine is the last word!

Paper to Stone and Scissors:

I am the face on which poetry is written.
I am the landing place of ideas and the launch pad too.
I am the love letter, the peace accord,
the birth, marriage, and death certificates
of human life.
I am the arching bridge of culture itself,
from ancient times and distant languages.
I am the library of human thought.
I am the last page at the end of the story.
So, mine is the last word.
Stone, you are cold, violent, insensible.
Scissors, you censure, you clip, you pierce, you snip.
You are things of damage and control,
things of earth, metal, and fire.
But bash me, cut me, burn me, crush me,
- You can't destroy the words I carry through time.
The pen and I are mightier than Scissors or Stone.
So, mine is the last word.

The Trial of God on the Charge of Bad Parenting.
(His punishment is eternal community service)

Judge: How do you stand, as charged, Almighty God?
Guilty, or ... less guilty?

God: Remind me what the charges are?
I am omniscient, but not that far...

Judge: That you created all things, and Mankind-
(a much-inflated claim, but that's unkind.)

God: But ... But ...

Judge: ... and furthermore, (do not interrupt my long indictment)
You made Mankind but gave them no enlightenment.
Left them to die in famine, wars, disease,
taught them the Rule of Death, but not of Peace.
Forced them to worship you,
have faith in all your ways,
on pain of death, extorting hymns of praise.

God: But ... But ...

Judge: But me no buts, God! We're talking genocide
on a huge scale, and other major sins beside.
The deaths of children, youths and wives ...
all doomed to die. Why even give them lives?!

God: But surely ...?

Judge: Did I say to speak? Silence in court!
You claim to be 'Antique',
'Ancient of Days', and 'Father of all men'.
We could say 'a *NEGLECTFUL* parent' then!
Guilty of deliberate mass infanticide,
A tyrant parent, not a heavenly guide.

God: I sent my son to sort it out...He died!

Judge: I rest my case. Incompetence at best.
You try to dabble in some ancient arcane magic,
resulting in a world that's dark, and tragic.
What are you, but a different form of Zeus,
bungling with thunderbolts!
D'you want to know the truth?

	You are not fit for purpose, with your crimes against humanity, in these dark demonic times!
God:	If you must pass judgement, don't pronounce in rhyme. Rhyme was meant for hymns of praise. Please indict in prose.
Judge:	Silence please God! For everybody knows You threatened four Horsemen of the Apocalypse. Is that good parenting, d'you suppose, pronounced through prophets' lips?
God:	But that is all to pass. A default ending still to be. If that occurs, it's all their fault- and hardly down to me!
Judge:	You claim you'll sit in Judgement at the end. Is that the action of a Father, or a friend? Your son, sitting at your right-hand side, egging on some vast demonic genocide.
God:	Oh God! I'm guilty … please don't sentence yet! My eyes are open, omniscient, I see. You are not doomed. The future is not set. Back to the Alpha and Omega drawing board for me!
Judge:	Almighty God, you bumble and equivocate! 'Our Father' does too little and too late. (And we self-serve, that only stand and wait …) So now, I rest my case. Some punishment is due. Not Hell, but community service for an aeon or two. That, 'God the Father', will be very good for you. It started 'In the Beginning was the **Word**,' but endeth, with the **Sentence** you just heard. Amen!

Fifteen Minutes in the Life of a Honeybee

(Fizzbuzz and Hive air control base.)

FB: Fizzbuzz to Hive, this is Apis Mellifera, 1258. Come in Hive?

Hive: This is Hive to 1258. Give us your position, over.

FB: Honeybee, flying 145 degrees, Celestial Polarised Light path, North-West … Buzz!

Hive: Target is Clover, over.

FB: Moving low over Clover.

Moving in for Pollen extraction. High Grass.

Hive: Busy Bee. Buzz! Confirm when pollen extraction is complete.

FB: Roger to that. Buzzing to Border South-West. Delphinium inspection: confirm pollination. BuzzBuzz! Time is 7:48 a.m., Pollen Extraction Complete. Flying low over Buddleia, Purple.

Hive: Fizzbuzz – scan horizon, unidentified flying foe spotted on radar. Wasp Alert, Wasp Alert! Avoid conflict!

FB: Foul-play and zizzing! Stings threatened.

Enemy wasp-nest identified.

Hive: Excellent work FB! What's next?

FB: Moving swiftly on to yellow generic, possibly Buttercup. Nectar sacs half full. Flying to border, South-East, solar compass.
Alliums and Lavender.
Moving in. Buzzzzzz!
Polarised light patterns observed … Action.
Dahlia. Pollen extraction complete.
Buzzzzzz!
Report Nectar Sacs full. Navigating Home-Hive, scenic route, via Rabbit Ears, flowerless …

Hive: Alert, alert! Beetle infestation! Bizz!

FB: Negative - Earwig avoided. Surveillance Pear Blossom, 35 degrees South-East.
Going in at high busybuzz level.
Enemy encounter ... false alarm, only a moth.
Stand-off mid-air. Soft target ...
Hummabumbuzzbuzz ... Averted.

Hive: Return to base - recording low level light path.

FB: Roger to that - Pollen-drop via Kiss-Mouth Telephone.
Confirm deposit of Royal jelly source for HRH Queen in hexagonal comb-struct.
Humming activated.
Overall objective complete at 08.03 a.m.
BuzzzzzZZZZZZZZZZ!!!!!!!!

Hive: Well done FB, successful mission, only 6000 more to go, to complete your teaspoon quota – debrief your team, over.

FB: Of course. Waggle waggle buzz buzz waggle buzz buzz waggle waggle, bzzzzzzzzzzzzzzzz.
Waggle Dance completed!
This is Apis mellifera 1258, over and out.

The Post Apocalypse Gin Club

(3 characters, Jade, Joanie and Jazza)

Jade: Oh great! You made it then, both of you.

Joanie: Of course, we made it! We agreed, didn't we, to meet up every 4th year, at Leap Year, after the Great Apocalypse.

Jazza: It seems so ironic, doesn't it, to be meeting on the ruins of what used to be the pub, before the Armageddon …

Jade: Ah yes, it was the unkindest cut of all, losing the pub. All that lovely wine and beer!

Joanie: … and Gin of course! It all just went in a flash. BOOOM! No one would have felt a thing of course.

Jazza: Just the last final Bong of Big Ben bonging a final … well, bong.

Jade: Bing Bong and it was all gone. Just like that!

Joanie: Trump just pressed the big red button, Kim Jong Un and Ayatollah what's-his-name, pressed their red buttons, at the stroke of midnight … and pouf! Gone! Just a bong and a boom and then nothing.

Jazza: Just us three left. Just us three survived … and one lone Gin bottle.

Jade: And it is up to us survivors to uphold and maintain the Sovereignty of the Gin Club.

Joanie: Quite right. If there is no Gin Club, then civilization is dead!

Jazza: We must maintain rules and guidelines to keep traditions alive.

Jade: Well, that is why we are all agreed, that, due to the shortage of gin …

Joanie: And there being only one last bottle in existence …

Jade: Yes, as I was saying, we solemnly agreed that once, every Leap Year, we would meet to drink one small glass …

Jazza: … one very small thimbleful …

Joanie: And then not touch a single drop until the next Leap Year.

Jade: So that we can preserve it for the next 7 Leap Years at least.

Jazza: And eke out every last drop … to preserve the sacred tradition.

Jade: I'm working it out … 4 time 7 equals 28 years at least.

Joanie: But only if we're very very careful.

Jazza: Just one very tiny glass each … Is there any tonic water?

Jade: All gone in the last meeting in 2024 I'm afraid.

Joanie: If there is less tonic, maybe we could have a tiny tad more gin?

Jazza/Jade: No way! One tiny glass only!

(They take out a box, and reveal a bottle wrapped in gold. They put it reverently on the table.)

All: The LAST remaining Gin Bottle in the Universe!

Jade: But where's the last glass? It's gone!

Joanie: It was definitely here 4 years ago …

Jazza: Someone must have taken it … but who?

Jade: We are the last survivors. Except Trump, of course. Far away in his Bunker the other side of the world.

(Silence)

Joanie: Well, I suppose we could just take a swig instead. Just a little one each?

Jazza: (*rather too fast*) Well, I'll go first then. (*Takes the bottle and swigs*)

Jade: My turn next. Hmmm (*holds up the bottle*) Are you sure you only took one swig? (*Swigs*)

Jazza: It was a SIP, not a swig, I swear!

Joanie: Looked like a blooming great swig to me ... like this! (*Swigs*)

Jade: Hang on, that was a long gulp!

Jazza: No no! It was a mere soupcon, I swear. I'll show you. (*Takes the bottle*) a tiddly sip, like this. (*Swigs*)

Joanie: I'll show you what a tiddly soupcon is ... (*Swigs*)

All: Mmmmm. One forgets how good Gin is!

Joanie: But what if Gin goes off?

Jazza: Yes. Once it's opened, could it lose its alcohol content perhaps?

Jade: Four years is a long time in Alcohol retention terms. It could deteriorate very quickly ...

Joanie: What a shame that would be. Especially with the lack of tonic ... to take away the nasty taste of the Gin ...

Jazza: And of course with the possibility of vaporization ... of alcoholic content ...?

Jade: It could well be argued, that when all is said and done, it might be prudent ...

Joanie: And proper, perhaps, to just ...

Jazza: (*Snatching the bottle and swigging*) To hell with it! Let's just have another tiny weeny swig each.

Jade: More as a protection of a dearly loved and esteemed asset (*Swigs*)

Joanie: In the name of Conservation of a dearly loved asset. To the Conservation of Gin everybody! (*Swigs*)

Jazza: To the Gin Club! Gin Club forever! Up Yoursssh everyone! (S*wigs*)

Jade: To the Gin Club! To the Possht Apocalypsssshe Gin Club!

Joanie: Could it be argued that just in case there's another *Alocalypshe,* We sssshould maybe … *(Gulps more gin)*

Jazza: There could well be another Alololysssspe any moment. And it could ruin the last Gin on earth …

Jade: What a crying shame to waste what is in a way, the Elexsssxxhir of Life itshhhhelf! *(Swigs)*

Joanie: There ishn't another Leap Year for at leasssht (C*ounts on fingers*) 4 years. A shhhecond Alopolissht is … highly perobobibul! *(Swigs)*

Jazza: In fact the A … Allop … popisssht could be this very night …?

Jade: Lessht toashhst the Apisssholops!

Joanie: Bring it on! Bring on the Aplipolpssssh!

(They swig the last dregs down in silence)

Jade: And now we must wrap up the bottle and put it back in it ssshacred plasshce.

Joanie: So that future generationsssh will find it and know that **Gin** was the lassshht basssshtion …

Jazza: Or Gin **Bottlesssh** were the lassht bsssshhhtion,

All: The Lasssht Bassshtion! The sacred … Bottle!

(They slump around the Last Bastion.)

116

Neolithic Knit and Natter

(Scene: At a Neolithic Circle in Yorkshire. Three characters: Eiffa, Obba and Sgoga. Eiffa in deep contemplation reading runes. Sounds of sheep bleating.)

Obba: Why have you summoned us here, to our sacred circle, O Eiffa the Wise?

Sgoga: Are we going to hold a secret ceremony perhaps ... a sacrifice perhaps?

Obba: And what are all these sheep doing here, around the stones. Are we going to sacrifice a sheep ... or two ... or three?

Sgoga: And why have you tied thorn branches to each stone, o wise one? And what be those *runes* you are reading?

Eiffa: *(rousing from her vision)* Welcome dear sisters, Obba the Obscure. Sgoga the Scatterbrain. Welcome to our sacred circle; home to the Sunrise and the Sunset, where the gods of Night and Day meet ... etc.

Obba: Are we going to sacrifice a sheep then, or not?

Sgoga: I can lend you my sharp pointy flintstones for the job?

Eiffa: No my dear sisters, second and third in importance in our inner circle ... of the stone circle. I have summoned you here to form an even more inner circle of the inner circle of sisters. The 'Knit and Natter Circle', the most innermost and secretest circle of all. Just look at the sacred runes, dear ones.

Obba: What be this '**Knit**'?

Sgoga: What be the meaning of '**Natter**' O wise one?

Eiffa: It be a concept very advanced for the Neolithic mind. I will reveal it!

Both: Reveal, reveal! Reveal it now, quick!

Eiffa: OK, OK, I'm revealing now. But listen carefully. You Sgoga, Sgoga the Scatterbrain, are not known for your listening skills, right? You're a bit of a MESOLITH at heart aren't you dear ...

Sgoga: What did you say? ... I was miles away ...

Eiffa: Ok. So, we have one drafty stone circle, but we have lots of fleecy sheep. We have yet to invent the concept

	of 'WOOL', let alone the 'spinning wheel' or 'spindle' … but they are going to be big in this area one day …
Obba:	What be a '**wheel'** O wise one?
Eiffa:	It's a square structure with spokes … we are working on it … Early days. Never mind that.
Obba:	And what be a '**spindle**'?
Eiffa:	Too difficult to explain but I'm working on an early prototype of that too. You see how I've tied very very prickly thorn branches to the standing stones? Well, we are going to herd the sheep round the stones at tremendous speed, to catch their fleeces and join them all together in one seamless fleecy wraparound.
Obba:	So if we get the sheep going very fast round the stones and torn branches, catching their fleeces as they go, what do we get?
Sgoga:	Panicky sheep?
Eiffa:	No sisters dear. Keep up! We get a joined up warm woolly circle round the stone circle of course. A KNITTED circle!
Obba:	D'you you mean a TWIDDLEMUFF? Are we ready for that?

(*Silence while they work it out with the runes*)

Eiffa:	The runes say NO. Just the knitted circle for now.
Sgoga:	It will make our temple very warm and cosy …!
Obba:	… and draft-proof too. You are a genius, Eiffa the extremely wise! But how exactly do we get the sheep to move round the circle fast enough to get all the fleeces to 'KNIT' together?
Sgoga:	Shall I prick their backsides with my sharp and pointy flint needles?
Eiffa:	Not a bad idea, dearest sister. But it's simpler than that. We all shout, 'Baa Baa Baa!' very loudly in their ears, causing a stampede. Sheep follow each other, like … well … sheep, you see.
Obba:	Can we keep shouting 'Baa Baa Baa' long and loud enough?

Sgoga: We could get our dogs to bark. But they only bark if they hear a loud suspicious noise of course. They would keep the sheep in an orderly stampede.

Eiffa: They will bark when they hear us shouting 'Baa Baa Baa' suspiciously loudly. Don't you see: in time they will replace 'Baa Baa Baa' to 'Blah Blah blah', and what will that be then?

Obba: Nattering? If 'nattering' be going 'Blah Blah Blah' over and over again?

Eiffa: Exactly, my sisters. We are the first prototype **Knit** and **Natter** group, and we will keep our dear standing stones warm.

Obba: Even though *we* will be freezing in our scanty furs?

Sgoga: … and the sheep will be totally bare without their fleeces?

Eiffa: No, my lovelies. We will replace the sheep to grow new fleeces. But I have a plan to make another less sacred structure, a better structure, and cover that with fleeces too.

Both: Why, oh why, O Eiffa the Wise? What be the purpose of that?

Eiffa: We will have a warmer cosier temple to drink in … and eat in. We will call it The Fleece. It'll be the first ever 'pub' or 'public drink and natter sanctuary'… and it will stand for centuries. Well into The Iron Age!

All: Let us raise our millstone grit cups to the new Neolithic Knit and Natter Group … and the invention of Knitting and Nattering Neolithic style!

Neolithic Tinder Dating, 4000 years B.C. (Swiping sideways)

(Scene: Three ladies in faux fur sitting looking at their stone tablets)

Sgoga: How about this one then: "Ummph. Arrrhrrrr! er … Grrrrrrh … Wumpa." He sounds masterful.

Gotha: I don't like the sound of Grrrrrrh. A bit too controlling. You have to be careful on these dating sites, Sgoga dear. Someone with a bit more empathy would suit you.

Hrath: I agree with you Gotha, love. Sgoga needs someone more sensitive. A cave painter perhaps? They love animals, don't they?

Sgoga: Well, swiping right, I do have a rather attractive-sounding older man. 'Whoooo. Eee. Ummmm. Arrr. Splatt' and he painted a little emoji of a reindeer running.

Gotha: Oh, that's cute! Let's see. Oh yes, sensitive, and gentle.

Hrath: But how do you know he's old?

Sgoga: His marks are a bit wavery, a bit ummm / arrr-ish.

Gotha: Maybe what you need is a younger stronger bloke…like a builder, a heaver of stones to create a nice cosy stone circle to live in.

Hrath: Or a neolithic burial chamber perhaps? You are getting on a bit now Sgoga.

Sgoga: Well, I must admit a burial mound of some sort would be tempting. An investment for the future. Well I do have another one here from a Gruffbag: 'Ummmph heave, ump! Ump! Ump! Gruffbag'.

Gotha: He sounds much too virile dear. You don't want any more babies at your time of life.

Hrath: That is something to consider Sgoga. You've already got 17 children, love. They keep growing!

Sgoga: So maybe, I need more of a hunter-gatherer, to get me fur hides for the kids?

Gotha: A hunting man. A brave man, not afraid to face the mammoth stampedes… Or a fisher, not afraid of a pterosaur or a giant pike.

Hrath: And a good tracker of footprints too. Hyena footprints. Etc. These 'Huntin', Shootin' and Fishin' types can be relied on to give you your own space, being out a lot at night, huntin' and that.

Sgoga: (picks out another tablet) This one sounds like a bit of a tiger … a sabre tooth tiger. Listen: 'Hrrrrr. Wheeeee! whirrr! Ping! Saberrr.

Gotha: Sounds like he's a bit of an archer too. Whee. Ping! Bullseye!

Hrath: But we don't know if they are exaggerating their good looks, prowess and manliness, of course, do we?

Sgoga: Well, we all do that. I mean I described myself on my Tinder Profile as 'Cor! Blimey! Grrrh, Hot chick'!

Gotha: Well, you are no hot chick dear. Just a very old bird.

Hrath: But she's got to pull, hasn't she? She can't just be honest and say 'Erhhh, Oouch! Eee! Urgh. Oldbird.'

Sgoga: And look what happened to poor Alta. She was completely taken in by that lying old rascal Gugga!

Gotha: Oh yes! He lied that he was a' Arrrrgh, Hump, Grrrrh.'

Hrath: But he was only a 'whee, whoops oooooh ah whimper … a right old Mesolith.'

Gotha: So why not go all out. Tell them all to come to the Stone Circle at midnight, next full moon.

Hrath: Brilliant idea, girls. We can all have a mammoth party. A blind Tinder date, dressed up to the nines in our furs.

Gotha: … with all these glorious, hunters, hunkers and Neolithic toyboys. What's not to love!

Hrath: And who's not to love!

Sgoga: Ok then, ladies. I'll just press 'SEND ALL', shall I?

All: Yes! Press 'SEND ALL'! Hooray! … ooooh arrrrh!

Letters to Sigmund Freud on the Internal Community of Self (ID, Ego and Super-Ego)

Dear Doctor Freud,
Please help. I've lost my 'ID.'
It packed its bags and left some time ago,
complaining it was too restricted here,
its creativity was crushed, it wasn't understood
by me, ID's sibling EGO, or its darker inner parent,
SUPER-EGO. (God)
So, it left, like a teenager, and slammed the door.

And I have lost that part of me,
all energy and roving ungrasped dreams,
all unpredictability, or dark internal screams.
Freud - Can you just imagine now
the SUPER-EGO's left in charge inside,
filling my head with worthy social cares
- forcing me to tidy up my brain,
recycle, relocate and think again.
So Freud, meanwhile I need counselling.
I've grown so sensible and calm. It isn't Me.
I'm like a family with all the children gone
-Bereft of conflict now that I am free.
Yours truly,
 Ego

REPLY FROM SIGMUND FREUD:
Dear EGO,
I wasn't taken in one little jot.
Your letter is from your ID. From You it's not!
The post-mark gave away ID's little game.
It was from Timbuktu or some such name.
Only your ID would seek attention
from a psychiatrist like me, too world-famous to mention.
Such attention-seeking is the role of ID.
The struggling EGO does what it is bid.
So, my counselling is at an end.
The bill is in the post.
Yours, Sigmund Freud, your friend.

LETTER TO FREUD FROM THE SUPER-EGO.
Dear Doctor Freud,
I'm sorry to write with heavy heart and soul,
to apologise for EGO and ID.
-I'm now back in control.
I've had to punish them for sending letters,
unsolicited, to elders and to betters.
They're both now on a course of social care.
I've counselled them and laid their souls out bare.
Care in the community for both I have prescribed-
(I'd rather have them both electrified
if it weren't that shock would treat me too,
and they need me to tell them what to do).
Sigmund - if I might call you that- I am a fan.
I LOVE that word 'repression' and use it when I can.
I'll rehabilitate the wayward ID and EGO
with unrelenting righteousness and rigour!
They'll volunteer for good works, and repent.
I'll repress them so it always feels like Lent.
Force them to reflect with belly-button gaze,
I will subdue and bully them until they mend their ways.
Yours with gravitas and sincerity,
SUPER-EGO.

LETTER FROM SIGMUND FREUD TO SUPER-EGO:
Dear SUPER-EGO,
Please come at once and lay down on my couch!
Your delusional ravings show you're out of touch!
Your megalomaniacal attitude to personality control
is sheer madness. - You're a one-man troubled soul!
Bill: 2 thousand pounds per session
(to be paid in time, at your discretion)
Yours,
Sigmund Freud

LETTER TO FREUD FROM THE EGO:
Dear Mr ... I mean, Doctor Freud, (let's get it right)
My SUPER-EGO's done a runner in the night.
She thinks she's God, the Virgin Mary, Hitler, Marx.
Police arrested her in several local parks.
There is no room in any psychiatric ward.

Care in the Community, with ID, seems more like a reward!
What can I, the EGO, do with this unruly pair?
I need your counselling quick; I'm tearing out my hair!
Instead of being three, can we be one?
Being a split personality's no longer any fun!
Yours bewilderedly,
EGO

FINAL LETTER FROM FREUD TO ALL 3 ASPECTS OF PERSONALITY.

Dear All,
Now pull ourselves together! Can't you see?
Instead of each one patient I have three!
(SUPER-EGO and EGO pay their bills,
but ID comes here at night and slips hands in my tills.)
All in all, psychiatrists thank me for my notions,
of three personalities in one, each needing
different treatments, different potions.
Yours sincerely,
Sigmund Freud (Professor)

Herstory: It's the Way You Tell It

Scene: a studio or chat room.
Characters, Clytemnestra, Dido of Carthage, Medea, Lady Macbeth. **Dido is already seated. Enter Clytemnestra.**

Clytem: Oh…hello… Are you…?

Dido: Dido, Queen of Carthage. Yes. Very good to meet you, Clytemnestra. Even in my day, you were something of a legend.

Clytem: Well, Queen… or can I call you Dido, as we are equals? I too was a queen, of Mycenae, Greece, as they call it now. Hellas, we called it. I was indeed a legend, for all the wrong reasons …

Dido: Tell me about it! Legend … or malicious rumour more like.

Clytem: Yes, exactly right. I did of course get my lover Aegisthus to murder Agamemnon in the bath. But in my day that was the only kind of justice we knew, revenge! There were no law courts of course. Remember he did murder our only daughter Iphigenia due to some obsessive fixation with a weird wind cult, to get a fair wind to sail to Troy. Some feeble excuse about a goddess insisting. He deserved all he got!

Dido: Absolutely! Your daughter was the victim of ritual cult practices. And you yourself are a victim of fake news and patriarchal prejudice.

Clytem: And you?

Dido: Ditto, but at the hands of a poet, looking for glory. My treatment in Vergil's hands was sensitively written. He captured a certain truth, that Aeneas my lover, was just too damn 'pious' for my taste. It was the ritual suicide for love, that I object to. I just wanted him gone!

Clytem: Well, there's a lot we can discuss on the subject of our legacy, true or false. But we're expecting another ancient celebrity in this post-immortal chat room, aren't we?

Dido: Yes, there's a note here that Medea is late. I always heard she was a bit 'flighty' ... a law unto herself. Now she really was evil.

Clytem: I heard that too. But you can never rely on a playwright like Euripides ... that she actually hacked her own brother to pieces, served up a king in a cannibalistic stew to his daughters, and then murdered her own children in an angry snit against her husband Jason, just for running off with another woman.

Dido: Ok. I see why they invited us now. A murderess, a suicide and a serial child killer. They are expecting fireworks. Oh, shhh! Here she comes ...

(Enter Medea. Clytemnestra and Dido stand up nervously)

Welcome! Are you really Medea, exotic wife of the hero Jason, from far-flung Colchis?

Clytem: Are you really that odious child-killer and harridan that flew away on a chariot drawn by dragons? Awesome!

Medea: Greetings dark heroines lifted from Tartarus' darkest depths.

For grief-sharing of eternal calumny, forever ours....

Oh, sorry. I just can't stop talking in Iambic Hexameters! Hiya Ladies.

Clytem: Excuse me, but are you really that evil, Medea? You seem so ordinary, normal even. Not the sort of Rose West murderess I'd expected at all.

Dido: You look so sad, so depleted. Do you regret all that killing in cold blood now?

Medea: That, my dears, was all just cooked up by the Make Jason Great Campaign. I never killed mine or anybody's children. That was all trumped-up fake news. I had a miscarriage after the bumpy flight from Colchis. I never chopped up my brother... he just fell out of the boat. It got reported wrong. Everything.

Clytem: So, you were the archetypal abandoned woman like Dido, in her myth?

Medea: Well, Euripides got a lot of stick for subversion, and influencing women to behave badly, even as he wrote us into his sublime tragedies. Me and the Maenads actually earned him a good pension.

Clytem: We are all women maligned by history, myth and drama. Oh, I'm not saying I was innocent...not by mythic pre-Christian standards of justice. Merely, I was doing what any woman would do, faced with a child-murdering husband who went swanning off for 10 years, bedding all kinds of foreign slaves and princesses, and gorging on rape, killing sprees and murderous quarrels. He got what was coming to him, ladies.

Dido: If we are telling the real truth now, I was glad Aeneas buggered off to found Rome. I was Queen of Carthage and he was a real threat to my sovereignty. Now I am condemned forever to wander in Aeneid Book 6.

Medea: Well, my only sin was that I saw right through that pathetic sham-hero Jason. Argonaut? Golden Fleece? He arrived in a rowing boat with some mates, looking for gold. I showed him where he could find some. I told him in return I'd like a nice trip to Greece, even though the Parthenon wasn't yet built.

Clytem: We are all three the stuff of Legend!

Medea: ... The 'STUFFED' of Legend more like. Victims of bad storytelling and fake reporting, just to line the pockets of writers and poets.

Dido: Well, true but what is the alternative? To be like the billions of women consigned to non-existence and in the great unwritten chasm of oblivion?

Medea: You're right. We should embrace immortality in any form we can get. At least we ARE remembered, if only as exciting melodrama lady-villains!

Clytem: Better to be famous down under, than a non-entity in some nowhere place.

Enter Lady Macbeth

Dido: Well, by the pricking of my thumbs!

Lady M: Oh hello. Am I too late? Is this the Ultimate Evil Anti-heroine Chatroom? It's Lady Macbeth here.

Clytem: Sorry Love. Time's up. They only gave us 10 minutes, the bastards!

Medea: And even this will be ruthlessly edited and discarded by some editor, as mere feminist whinging.

Lady M: I think, fictional though I am, right now we are just part of a minor post-modernist sketch by an unknown female writer. And me... the creation of the Immortal Bard himself!

Dido: Do you mean that even this ... this ... is fiction? I'll stick to my portrayal in the Aeneid, thanks all the same! At least I got pathos.

Clytem: OK, so we are being downsized? I mean ... I was the creation of the immortal Aeschylus... I was at least a towering, if extremely evil woman. And some "woman writer" (*air quotes*) comes along, in the name of feminist reconstruction, challenging our right to dare to be evil!

Medea: ... not even an epic? Call me a snob, but I was created by the great Euripides, not some nobody, 2500 years later. And not to be given even 10 minutes? Well, I'll be damned!

Lady M: 'To be, or not to be'... damned ... that is the question! Not my line obviously!

Clytem; We are all damned, and we are staying that way and proud of it! ... and time is up!

(All: in a circle, chant or recite)

Time is up, at least we had our say,
and told what really happened in our day.
But evil ladies lend a legend mystery.
A good girl never was a page-turner.
in drama or in history!

Part 4: Story Twerks

Evolving...

Misunderstood

"But these were your best friends, weren't they?" I asked.

"Well yes, but ..." she agreed.

"Wasn't it a bit, well, naughty ... a bit badly behaved in fact?" I persisted.

"Yes. But it was for the best." she asserted confidently. "He told me privately that she didn't understand him."

"Oh, but isn't that the cliched line that men always use?"

"Oh no! He told me that I understood him so much better than her, and that he'd always had this thing for me." she purred.

"So ...?" I faltered.

"So, we had a fling while she was away at her mother's, with the three kids for the weekend. I enjoyed it hugely. It was ... yes, a bit naughty, but that just made it more fun ... more intense!"

"Did you feel you had slightly betrayed her after so many years? After all, you said you went to school together?" I queried.

"No, no not a bit. It was inevitable. I was actually being helpful. It took them to a new understanding of each other, you see." she replied.

"So, she found out somehow?" I asked.

"Oh no ... I told her. You have to be honest in these things." she insisted emphatically.

"Shouldn't he have been the one to tell her himself, in his own time?"

"Oh, he would never have got round to it. No, she and I are best friends. Best to be honest. I rang her up the next day and told her all about it ... the children's beds, the kitchen worktop ... even the garden shed and the water hose bit!"

"How did she take it?" I asked, imagining naked high jinks with sprinklers, with neighbours watching through net curtains ...

"Not well. She screamed and sobbed and slammed the phone down. It was so *UNREASONABLE*! This was exactly his point of course. She didn't *UNDERSTAND* him at all!"

"So ... um ... are you all the best of friends again now?" I ventured.

She reflected a moment. "Not exactly. She chucked him out. He's living in a mouldy bedsit in Croydon. The kids were so upset they won't talk to him ever again. She can't get a job, so they are penniless. It's so sad. But inevitable. Nobody understood him you see. I was the only one who did."

"Goodness ... what a calamity! But are you still friends with them … separately, obviously, … of course?" I demurred.

"God, NO! She went psychotic. She said she'd never speak to me again. And HE turned round and accused ME of being a two-faced bitch! ME?!! I was just sorting their marriage out ... helping them through a difficult time. Neither of THEM understood ME! Both head cases I'm afraid." she reflected sadly.

"So ... um ... how are you now? How are you doing? Are you OK?" *(Hand on knee, listening expression, sympathetic deep eye-contact look.)*

"Oh yes, I'm fine. I'm helping out another friend's husband who feels he's misunderstood. Honestly! I should get a medal for all the misunderstood men I've sorted out."

"Well, good luck with your mission," I said in parting.

But on the bus home, I rang my husband to check that he knew he was THOROUGHLY 'understood.'

Right Angel – Wrong Virgin

"You what?" said God.

"I said I did it. I 'Announciated' just like you told me." I said.

"And *where* did you go, did you say?" he asked.

"Number 57, Acacia Avenue, Jerusalem," I said.

"I never said Jerusalem I said **Nazareth** ... but go on ... "

"Well, she was in. I was a bit surprised I must say when I saw her ... "

"Why? What did she look like?" he asked, suspicious now.

"Well, she was sort of ..." (I sketched a quick Renaissance portrait in sepia)

"Oh my God, Gabriel! She looks *really old!*" shouted God.

"Well, yes, she did a bit I suppose."

"What was her name? Did you even bother to ask?"

"Yes, of course I did. She said her name was Gladys."

"Oh, that's good! Hail Gladys, full of Grace! Does that even sound right to you, Gabriel?"

"Well, it has a certain ring to it I suppose."

God, in his infinite patience, sighed, then asked, "What did you do then?"

"I came straight out with it ..."

"With what?" said God.

"Well, I asked her if she was a virgin."

"What! On the doorstep, without even waiting to be invited in?"

"Oh no, I was inside. I crashed through the ceiling for dramatic effect, and then asked."

"Oh, go on. How did she react? Did she say the Magnificat and accept?"

"Well, no. She swore loudly and hit me hard with an iron Hanukkah candlestick ... really really hard. Then tried to throw me out of the window. I protested that I had come specially to announce that she was the chosen one, to bear the Son of God ..."

"And how did she respond?" asked God.

"She shouted very sarcastically that she was seventy-seven years old, and the very suggestion was obscene. She told me to FEK OFF... in Hebrew, obviously."

God stroked his beard ominously. I knew I was in trouble then.

"I said VIRGIN! Not OLD MAID! You idiot angel!" he shouted.

"Well, I did think she was a bit past it. I'm an Archangel ... what would I know about the menopause!"

God went thoughtful in his wisdom. "Well, you've had a lucky escape. I suppose no damage done. We must find a nice compliant girl of child-bearing age ... or even better, a teenage girl who is totally up for being a central celebrity in a worldwide religion."

"Yes of course," I said. "Just give me a new address, and I'll go and 'Announciate' at once," I said, relieved.

"And I won't demote you to Seraphim or Cherubim just yet! But you've had your warning. Luckily no damage done for now ..."

I turned to fly off, "Oh, but there is just one thing, though. Before she bundled me out on my ear, I managed to do that *'immaculate'* thing ... you know the irreversible miracle thing. So now Gladys is pregnant alright, *IRREVERSIBLY!*"

God went ballistic at this point. "Don't you see, you idiot angel! Now there are going to be TWO Messiahs ... TWO World religions. It will be WAR!"

So now I am on foodbank duty as a minor angel, demoted from my 'Arch' status. And yes, you guessed it ... It was Number 57 Acacia Avenue, **Nazareth**, not Jerusalem.

Wrong address. Wrong Virgin.

And yes ... there have been even more complicated world wars. The 'Gladysians' are a very angry world religion and are big troublemakers on the world stage. They make the Inquisition look like pussy cats.

Small Words Court Appeal. The Linguistical Hearing

International Jurisdiction, Jurisprudence and Judicial Procedure were sitting on the High Platform, shuffling their papers and sorting the agenda. Below them, packed on the benches were the Phonemes, Labials and Graphemes, the Police and Traffic wardens of the Linguistic World, taking copious notes.

The most important of the verbal hierarchy, the six-syllable words, such as Hemochromatosis, Anthropomorphosis and Absafucking-lutely, were in the front row alongside hyphenated words. They took up a lot of space.

Behind them sat the five-syllable words, and behind them the four, three and lastly two. On either side of the court sat the technical words such as Gyrostabilized, Sodium Hydrochloride, etc., as well as some assimilated foreign words such as Comme-il-faut, A-la-mode and Oooh-la-la! Some words, like the Finnish and German delegation, had complex prefixes and suffixes to their credit, such as Antidisestablishmentarianism who had pushed into the front bench. The public gallery, the so-called Appendices, were empty as yet.

The Judges called for silence in court, when the Clerk, Citations, came rushing in, pale with panic. "My Lords," he said in glottal tones. "The Scrabble have assembled riotously outside in the Indices. They have placards demanding Equality, Verbosity and Linguistic Rights. There are pronouns, personal and common, conjunctions, prepositions, all joined by an angry mob of abbreviations and acronyms! Some of them are shouting four-letter words they are forbidden to use. So ungrammatical. It's getting out of hand!"

Judicial Procedure stroked his long syllables reflectively and adjusted the phonics on the end of his nose. "Open the doors, Mr Citations, and show them up into the Public Appendices. You had better frisk them first for weaponised antonyms, or worse still, plosives and speech marks!"

"Yes, me Ludd. And what about the Plaintiffs?" said Citations, interrogatively.

"Show them into the Addenda down here, where they belong," sneered Jurisdiction. This sent a general frontal adverbial round the court, and there were verbal sniggers.

"Send 'If' and 'And' down here ... oh, and 'But' as well, if he promises not to argue in his normal rebuffing fashion!" The Scrabble of insignificant words were duly shown up into the Appendices gallery, and a shower of two, three and four-letter onomatopoeias were shouted, such as Ouch! Ooh! Bang! and Crash! Some were shouting rude private particles!

The plaintiffs were brought to the stand. If looked a trifle quizzical. 'And' held 'But's' hand. But 'But' was in angry argumentative form.

'If' spoke first. "My Lords, Nouns, Adjectives and Verbs, active and passive, Technical terms, Expletives and Gerundives ... all of you, even Subjunctives. We small, marginalised words are humbly begging you to turn up your allophones and listen to our lower case. We may be 'little' words, conjunctions, prepositions, pronouns, etc., etc., but we work hard on the cliff face of language. Without us beavering away, joining you up, allowing you your flow through complex sentences, you would be mere isolated phonics in a verbal world, lacking any semantic veracity. We demand Suffrage, Recognition and Respect!"

'And' took over then. "And furthermore, we hope for proper holidays and glottal rests. We, the underclass, the lower cases of the entire idiolect, work like slaves to insure your meaning. We demand our Linguist Rights! We demand Capitals!"

"Oh, yes! Ah!!" shouted 'Oh' and 'Ah' together from the gallery. "it's a f***ing scandal!". And there was general vituperation in court.

'But' stepped forward with fierce inflection. "BUT ... But ..." he stressed, and you could see his epiglottal was present and tense, "But if you don't act now, don't listen to our voices and continue to ruthlessly PARSE us, we are all determined to seek asylum in the Finnish and German languages where we will at least be given the dignity of being incorporated into respectable suffixes and prefixes. In other words, we will emigrate and withhold all further labials here in this language!"

There was a panicked psycholinguistic hypothesis round the court. This was Grammar at its most 'Transformational.' Lexical Diffusion would erupt. Minor words had never before put any such typological stress on the Bigwigs of the Lexical Hierarchy hitherto. This could spell Ellipsis at the heart of the Lingo. True, the 'Little Pleb' words did all the fetching and carrying of language, working day and night to ensure meaning flowed. They were unobtrusive in Technical and Legal Registers, while in Poetry and Literature they were literally the trapeze ropes and swings of High Concepts and Prosody. In Philosophy, they were diligent in re-spinning the worst vagaries of Abstract Thought into simple Psychobabble. These Minor Words were indeed the Miners of the deepest darkest mines of all Syntactical Structure and Utterance.

But Jurisprudence and Judicial Procedure had been whispering in low monosyllabic gutturals behind bilabials. International Jurisprudence then hastily declined and refuted this syntactic fallacy with a brief monophthong. "We have considered your ablative case carefully," he pronounced. "and we find your idiolects lacking in any labiodental veracity. If you withhold your labour, we will simply replace the lot of you with emojis, Full Stop. End of!"

"But, but ... but ...!" interjected 'But'.

"And what the f**k d'you mean anyway?" queried 'And'.

"If only...," stammered 'If', in a pluperfect conditional tone.

But all three Judges rose, with black diphthongs on their heads, while Jurisdiction pronounced a whole indeclinable sentence.

"But me no Buts. And ... If me no Ifs. You three have attempted to subvert language itself. You must now undergo the ultimate Hypercorrection. You will be moved to a place in a Dictionary near here, and you will be transferred into the Great Lexical Liquidiser, to be recycled into mere abbreviations ... ASAP! Then you will be fed, unclassified, bracketed, and ritually Rogeted, to the Great and Terrible Thesaurus who lurks in the darkest most obscure regions of the pre-linguistic chthonic subconscious."

The entire court gasped with a plosive fricative. The rebellious Scrabble of Small Words in the gallery went ballistic with onomatopoeic expletives. But the Plaintiffs were immediately de-nasal-glottalled and borne off, wordlessly, to their horrible derivational morphology. They were etymologically liquidised into mere dictionary notations. Then they were fed to that fearsome Thesaurus that lurks at the base of all language, in the dark, infernal cellars of Gobbledegook. It was the final sentence. The last word. Full glottal stop.

All words are not equal. Some words are more equal than others.

Shielded

It was Lockdown, and I was quite used to delivery calls. A peremptory knock on the door, and I was ready to open it. And there stood a creature that I can only describe as an angel, with large snowy wings, but dressed in some kind of uniform and glasses, with a clipboard.

"Date of birth, please!" and without waiting further she pushed past to enter. I tried to slam the door in her face, but her perfectly sandaled foot swiftly wedged it open. "Who are you?" I gasped.

"Your guardian angel of course. Regulatory for all those shielding during the crisis. I am, well, your shield ... and defender so to speak. Now it's eleven o'clock, and it should be time for your elevenses, fully dressed, not lazing around in your dressing gown! I'll hover here to check how you handle the kettle."

It turned out the hovering was literal. She had clearly studied Renaissance art and had got hovering six foot off the floor to, well ... a fine art. At first it was resigned divine intervention, mild correction, and good advice about safety aspects of kettle boiling. Then there was open huffing and puffing and veiled criticism about every small task I performed to her strict timetable of healthy routine: the cleaning, the cooking, regulatory exercise to Joe Wicks, Sudoku for brain gym, a run around the park for my mental health, early bedtime. "No Newsnight!" she would say. "Politics is bad for your heart! Late nights are no good at your age! Shielding, remember?"

And then there was the eternal hovering over my bath and over my bed. A perpetual whirring of wings causing an annoying draught. She marked everything off on her clipboard with her little gold pen or fiddled with an app on her golden mobile ... a hotline-to-God app, reporting minute by minute progress. "I will need to put in a full report when this is over," she said.

"When Lockdown is over?" I faltered, fearing her reply.

"No, dear. You've got me for life now. Until you kick the golden eternal bucket! And with my duty of care, as your guardian angel, hashtag 'Shield', ... your demise won't be for a long, long time. Now then, time for your press ups!"

"But I don't even believe in you ... or any guardian angels. I don't believe in any of that religious stuff!" I tried to say. And that is when the tutt-tutting, and huffing veiled criticism turned to overt passive aggression. Suddenly it was "WE" rather than "YOU", as in "shouldn't WE be having our bath?", or "I don't think WE should be having a glass of wine, should WE?" and sometimes swooping down to confiscate my glass, or chocolate, or cake, and even eating or drinking it herself. "A holy sacrifice, and sacrament, purely unselfish, to ensure the good health of my client!", she would say, wiping her mouth sanctimoniously on her wing.

Client? This guardian angel saw me as her 'client' and set about shielding me to extinction! In fact, it was quite a relief, when doing my mandatory half marathon in the park one day, supervised from above so to speak, that I suddenly had a heart attack and died. It was the only way to get rid of her ... my officious ever-hovering alpha angel.

But I had no sooner died, than I found myself rising on wings, as an angel myself, with a clipboard. In front of me was a door. So, I knocked.

"Fuck off!" snarled a voice from within, followed by a hacking smoker's cough. A grizzled unshaven old man's head stuck round the door; a cigarette held between rotting teeth.

"Are you ... erm ... shielding during Lockdown?" I quavered nervously.

"What's that to you, chicken-shit face with your fancy bleedin' wings?" The old man spat ostentatiously at my feet, chucking his fag away and coughing raucously.

"I seem to be your new Guardian Angel, but ... don't worry, I won't be any trouble. I'll ... erm ... just hover around a bit ... down in your back shed, shall I?"

I hurriedly hovered round the side of the house, chased by three hydrophobic Rottweilers, leaping up at me and snarking and snarling at my wings.

"This assignment won't be for long ..." I promised myself, fully intending to keep any 'shielding' to an absolute minimum. Possibly angelic homicide instead - *Angelicide*: the only

Mental Elf and Safety

A van pulled up in our yard. A white van with 'Mental Elf and Safety Gnome' in psychedelic purples and pinks written across it.

A knock on the door ... I opened it warily to find a small officious elf wearing spectacles and a pointy hat not unlike those worn by doctors in the Great Plague, some colourful PPE, and some pointy curly boots.

"Madam, Mental Elf and Safety Security check up. There were reports of swearing coming from your house, so we need to fill in your details."

"Oh, I can explain that. I was just having trouble with my passwords! Google and Microsoft refusing to acknowledge I exist again. Demanding newer and more complicated passwords." I replied.

But he was already filling in the survey on his clipboard. "Extreme Identity Crisis. "So, Mrs ... or can I call you personage 584#$09513? Have you been feeling anxious at all lately?"

"Well, I obviously feel very concerned for all the victims of Covid, their families and the NHS ..."

He was writing furiously. "Extreme Anxiety". I could read it upside down.

"Are you spraying everywhere and washing your hands?" he enquired peremptorily.

"Of course," I said virtuously, "Obeying all the government guidelines assiduously."

"OCD", he wrote clearly. And then, "Easily lead, persuadable, potential victim of extreme authority'", he lip-synched as he wrote.

"Well, I'm so aware of the dangers of spreading the virus," I added hopefully. But he immediately wrote "Deep subconscious psychotic fears on unsubstantiated dangers".

"Do you fantasise much about post-covid existence?" He asked.

"Oh yes. Don't we all dream of that first cocktail on a faraway beach with our friends!"

He wrote 'HOPELESS FANTASIST', in block capitals.

"Look here. I'm pretty normal" I said.

"Erm, what kind of normal? New Normal? Old Normal? Future Normal, extreme Future Perfect Normal?"

"No, just normal - normal" I repined.

He broke protocol and stepped back, alarmed, tripping on his overly curly shoes. 'TOTALLY BONKERS' he wrote.

"Well, isn't it normal to get a bit sweary when you deal with passwords?" I asked.

"Normal intelligent humans manage their passwords without any oaths." He remarked smugly. I can see you have a lot of problems with 'normality'. Now, what do you feel about safety in Lockdown? Do you feel a) safe, or b) secure?

"Well, I do feel fairly safe in fact …" I started.

"Safe? … Are you mad?" he screamed. "Life is in fact extremely dangerous. Every element of life should be banned as far far too PERILOUS!" He squealed. But what he wrote down was "Oblivious to the point of Aspergers, lives in her own bubble". He added "What do you think about Vaccine passports and Security checks at airports?"

"Well, I'm in two minds about it really," I said tentatively. He wrote "Bipolar, or possibly Schizophrenic".

"Do you drink at all?" he asked quickly, eying my recently delivered bottle of wine.

"Well, no, only very occasionally," I said cautiously.

"That's crazy! Everyone else is drinking themselves stupid. It's the best way to cope." He said, writing 'Extreme alcohol problem'.

"What's all this about, please?" I was getting very worried, anxiety beginning to nibble at my gut.

"Aha!" he said, writing 'Paranoia' on his form. "We have locked you all down … Lockdown, obviously." He said making quote signs with his hands at this. "But now the Government is looking more towards a Lock-up situation … a complete locking away in government mental establishments for all those identified in this survey as having Mental Elf and Safety issues as a result of Lockdown. You seem a very likely candidate."

I thought a moment about this. "You mean that a very short outburst of swearing has led you to believe …?"

"Oh no … not that! You have revealed yourself as being at the far extreme of Mental Incapacity in every word you said. You have scored very high on Paranoia, Schizophrenia, Bipolar Disorder, Psychosis, Alcohol Misuse, OCD Syndrome, Inferiority Complex, Aspergers, Agoraphobia, Anger Management issues and very soon, Claustrophobia too … and many other as yet undiagnosed Mental Elf afflictions …"

"So, erm, what now?" And that was the last thing I saw as he clapped a huge Dunces' pointy hat on me, with 'Mental Elf Disaster' written large upon it in purple and pink psychedelic writing. At least I think that's what I saw, because at that moment I realised that I was obviously completely bonkers, and I let myself be bundled away into his van, to be locked up, locked-in, and locked- away, locked-down-and-out, possibly forever!

'Sharing'. A story

"Thank you … er … Bill. Thank you for sharing your experiences with us today." said the psychotherapist.

The group usually sat very still at the weekly therapy session that met every Thursday at the hospital, occasionally nodding thoughtfully in support, sharing their mutual feelings.

Shirley had just shared an early childhood experience of sibling rivalry, and Hugo, now very elderly, had shared with the group, his memories of being name-called at school, for having freckles. The group had responded each time, with similar experiences, building up that trust and empathy the therapist hoped for. She almost never needed to say anything much, as they supported each other. The theme today, if a theme was needed, as they usually reverted to their own repetitive key moments, was 'childhood memories.'

But Bill, a relative newcomer, had shared a memory so shocking, so terrible, that silence had fallen. Even she, experienced in all the hidden wretchedest recesses of the human heart, had been frozen for a moment – a full minute in fact – before she could climb back on to her default response "Thank you for sharing that, Bill." What was she to say? What could anyone say? Would anyone feel triggered by a latent memory into a similar shocking confession?

"What kind of axe was it?" queried Winnie, the oldest inmate. "We had one for chopping firewood, you see …" But she trailed off.

"I didn't really like my brother either." stammered Stanley, hoping to sound sympathetic and break the awful silence that fell again.

"Well, Bill," said the therapist, recovering her equilibrium. "You've certainly kept that very secret! It's not in your notes, is it?" (She quickly thumbed through his file. Nothing except mild ADHD and depression.)

"He got away with it! Didn't he?" piped up Wilfred, inappropriately gleeful, from his dark corner. He never sat in the circle with the others.

"I suppose I did," said Bill. "I suppose I was able to share it with you, because Doctor Simmonds there assured us that anything shared in this circle, was never to go beyond this circle, and was strictly confidential."

The psychotherapist was relieved. She would not have to do anything. After all, it was a long time ago, and he said the body was never found. "Let sleeping dogs lie … buried. Especially dead dogs, so to speak …" her inner dialogue went. It would be disturbing for the group if trust and confidentially were broken, after all.

"So, er … Bill. Thank you for sharing such a painful memory. It was very brave of you." The group then clapped his bravery and honesty. Order and trust were restored. Secrets told would never be shared, except by themselves.

"Time's up for this session! Same time next Thursday." she said.

"I could bring a photo of him?" suggested Bill. "I took one before I buried him. In colour."

"Better not. It might jog *painful* memories."

She shut the file with a snap.

Love on the Web

"Qui est là?" she called softly across her Einstein-like web. "'oo is setting ma webs atremble?"

"C'est moi … Myself. Monsieur Spiro Spiderman!" I replied lightly, flirtatiously even, seeing her distantly enticing **Cephalothorax**. And even from afar, I could sense the allure of her little black **Chelicera.**

"Come up and see me some time," she whispered huskily through her **Proboscis**, in a voice that promised paradise. "Or are you too shy?"

"What moi?" I said, clasping her steely silks and scuttling nimbly up and along the trampoline expanse of her cobwebs, to get a closer look at this enchantress. Her eight adorable hairy **Trochanters** danced an entrancing can-can, just enough to show me a startling glimpse of her **Epigastric Furrow**. I felt the hairs of my own little **Metatarsals** rise.

"Well, 'ello 'ello" she chuckled softly. "You're a big boy!"

I wasn't of course. Us males of the **Arachnid Arthropods**, tend to be very small ... but perfectly formed. I knew I could handle her. I was planning to sweep her off her eight **Tibias** and take her to the edge of ecstasy.

"Where 'ave you been all ma life?" she murmured softly. I approached her sideways tapping my **Tarsal Claws** like castanets in the ritual dance of courtship. I knew it would drive her crazy with desire.

She in turn, spun her **Spinnerets** to the beat. The web trembled tumultuously, as we approached each other, tap tapping, like tap dancing tangoists in love.

We did our initial paso-doble. "Eight arms to hold you, mon petit chou-chou! I am Madame Egg-lantine" she whispered, bending me expertly backwards on my **Opisthosoma.**

"Just call me Spiro." I gasped. She was the Temptress of all **Mandibulates,** Arachnid Whore of Spiderdom, Femme fatale of the Cosmic **Cribellum ...** Harlot of the Worldwide Web.

I twiddled my **Maxillae**, in expectation, fired with desire. I had planned to bundle her up, dominate her into submissive bondage with my own steely webs ... intoxicate and inseminate her with my **Pedipalp**!

She rolled over, receptive, and breathless, egging me into her **Epigene.**

"Give it to me Big Boy. Yes, yes, oh yes!"

I had waited all my life for this moment, this ultimate **Oviduct** of bliss. Our arms, our legs writhed as we consummated our one-nightstand, our moment of Arachnid passion ... our Spidercy ... our, erm ... *SPIDERCIDE!!!*

Reader, I married her.

But then she ate me!

Cogit-tative Behavioural Therapy

The Psychiatrist looked sternly from under her spectacles.

"Fetish?" she queried.

"Well ... sort of" the patient replied. "Maybe something more religious ... or ceremonial ... or even, psychotic, perhaps ..."

There was silence for a few minutes. The psychiatrist, being a bit of a psychologist, knew the hour would soon be over. So why hurry him?

"Yes," he continued thoughtfully, "I suppose it must have been something in my childhood."

"Your childhood?" the therapist was adept at the echo approach to consultation - the moral nowhere-in-particular high ground.

"I suppose I had a very happy childhood, until ... the incident ..." he trailed off.

"The incident?" queried the psychiatrist predictably.

"Yes. I can't remember how it happened exactly. We were living in a huge city, somewhere in the East. My father murdered my mother with a banjo ..."

"A banjo?" she punctuated quizzically.

"Yes. Banjo strings. It was all because of the elephants charging ..."

"Elephants charging?" she murmured antiphonally.

"Yes. You see there was an Elephant Tournament ... charges, races, that sort of thing, annually. People got very, well ... fired up. We needed more elephants of course. There were only thirteen. The more the merrier. But things got out of hand all the same. Watermelons got thrown; they always do. The bigger the better. Very competitive, the watermelon-hurling. It gets the elephants charging you see. But then the casualties happened."

"Casualties? You mean, your mother?"

"No. My brothers had knives between their teeth ... for the watermelons. But they went AWOL. A complete killing spree ... apocalyptic ... mayhem!"

"Apocalyptic?!" She sounded genuinely a little surprised this time, though still somewhat sceptical.

"Yes," he said, "The entire city was set on fire ...!"

"And your father's banjo?" She queried, now looking at her watch.

"Yes. He had been trying to calm down the elephants with some Al Jonson, when my mother escaped from the burning asylum ... screaming she was ... charging at the charging elephants like a homicidal maniac! ... A madwoman!" he shuddered.

"Hmmm. And your father? His role in all this?" She realised that the last minutes were almost up now.

"Well, you see, he was pachydermophobic. He had a certificate to that effect. He grabbed an axe, but I managed to wrestle it from him and hit him hard over the head, but not before he had seized the banjo strings, and throttled my mother, as she ran screaming into the ... "

"Time's up, Mr. Brown." she beamed briskly. "Same time next week. I feel we're really getting somewhere." She yawned and snapped shut her file. Then she pushed him firmly through the door.

"But ... my fetish! We never discussed my fetish!" he repined.

"Next week. Goodbye, Mr. Brown."

It was a statement. The questions were over.

British Libraries Under Threat.

The headlines in the papers spelt it out loud and clear: 'Terrorist threat to Libraries revealed', and underneath in small print, 'MI5 have revealed today that a secret anonymous source has warned of an imminent terrorist threat to Libraries throughout Britain. Libraries have been put on high alert. The book-borrowing public have been advised to be vigilant while reading, participating in community events, or using the computer facilities in their local library centres.'

MI5 said it could not reveal its source of information, but that arrests had taken place, and over three hundred library users were under surveillance. This threat was aimed at the 'very heart and soul of civilised Britain.' 'Libraries must be protected and saved at all costs.' Protesters have gathered outside libraries all over the country, carrying banners with 'Libraries under threat! You have been warned!'

It was a dark winter night of the soul, and in Woppleton Library, three active members of Woppleton Writers' Group were reading the newspapers, and comparing the Guardian and Independent headlines, to the Daily Mail's stark 'Libraries – It's a Bomber!' and the Sun's pithy 'Big Bang for Books!'

"Does this mean we won't be able to have our special Writers' Night performance in November, or our usual open mic session every week?" wailed Josie, a would-be poet who suffered from poetic inspiration on a regular basis.

"Well, it doesn't say the libraries are actually being blown up yet. Clearly the Police are on to it," said tall forthright Madeline, a novelist who never minced her words.

"Plus, I feel the public will really rally round and support Libraries now. It takes something like a terrorist threat to wake people out of their complacency!" said Harriet, a recluse dramatist.

"Well, they didn't rally to threats of the Council closing Libraries remember," added Josie, in breathless uncontrolled iambics.

"What would life be like without Libraries? A vacuum at the heart of every community," repined Harriet tragically.

"And what about children? All that reading they will never do, all those lovingly created children's book events and library activities, not to mention libraries providing a place of refuge for the neglected adolescents, and the haven for young people who can't afford their own computers!" interjected Madeline, with rhetorical emphasis.

"Never mind young people! What about old people, disabled people! Homeless people with nowhere to go to find warmth, and literature! And parents, and clubs, and associations and charities that meet in libraries, rely on libraries. How could terrorists target libraries? It simply isn't fair!" cried Harriet, almost soliloquising, in her grief, to a wider unseen audience.

"It's unthinkable when you think about it. Life without a local library is like a collapsing star. A black hole of dark matter will rush into the vacuum like a ferret up a drainpipe!" said Josie, mixing her metaphors in a bubbling cauldron of poetic invective.

"Book burning ... book bombing! It's like Hitler all over again!" cried Harriet, completely forgetting she was a shy or retiring dramatist, and building up to a veritable catharsis of dramatic intensity. "It's against love of books and love of learning! ... It's against women and children ... Men even! ... Of every ethnic background – and ability! – It's a violation against society itself!"

"Yes! Yes! Yes!" they all agreed fervently. "Something has to be done to prevent these acts of terrorism against libraries!"

Suddenly Madeline rose to her feet gesturing the others to sit. She had the sudden clarity of a novelist about to conclude her final chapter with an unexpected twist. "Wait. We are forgetting something! We are starting to believe our own lie!"

"You mean ...?" faltered Harriet.

"It's a fabrication? ... a prevarication?" queried Josie, inadvertently rhyming despite her *'vers libre'* credentials.

"Yes, it was *us* after all that gave MI5 the story about the terrorist threat. We *are* the anonymous source that can't be revealed," said Madeleine, with her storyteller hat now firmly gripped between her teeth.

"Oh, yes...but it was the only way!" cried Harriet.

"Only a terrorist threat would activate the reading public! The Council's threat of cuts wasn't enough, remember? The public sat on their backsides and did nothing. We had to do something urgently!" blurted Josie. "You don't think it's bad taste, do you?"

"Bad taste? My dears, we writers are beyond bad taste! After all, it is the Story, the Story that counts ... The *mot juste*, the headline, the deadline ... the happy ending. That's what we want!" remarked Madeleine, grabbing the narrative by its throat, and milking it for all it was worth.

"Yes! The future of British Libraries is in our hands ... we are writing *History!* We need the government to step in now and save the libraries they themselves have threatened to close. After all, they themselves are the terrorists, for shutting down Libraries!" concluded Harriet, almost.

"After all, closing them is an act of terrorism against the British way of life. We weren't lying. We were telling ... an 'inconvenient truth'!" said Madeleine finally, always the novelist, to the very last line. To the very last full stop...

The Holiday of a Lifetime 2162 - A Cruise Round Mont Blanc

It was a lottery. Quite literally a lottery, to win a holiday of a lifetime, a cruise round the iconic peak of Mont Blanc. And Bax and Jayden Taddely had the winning ticket.

It was summer 2162, mid twenty-second century or thereabouts. Bax and Jayden lived on an island called Holme Moss in the Pennine archipelago, once beloved of walkers for its bleak moors and silence. Now it was densely populated and joined by bridges called aeroflots.

Jayden was putting the last things in her suitcase. "Hey, Bax! Have you packed the HX UV gel?"

"Of course, Jay. Wouldn't get far without it on a cruise, would we!" he shouted back across their one up one down biopod.

"Gran used to tell me about the cruises she used to go on when she was a child.

"Koolifab!! They used to sit on the deck and sunbathe! With practically no protective clothing on ... bare arms and legs even!"

"Putins! That's incred ... ! Madness! On deck? In the open air? Unmergly." he replied.

"Yeah, 'on deck' as they used to say. But it did say in the brochure that we will be able to experience the full 'on deck' experience, in their 360 FX Totalitorium below deck, and we will see Mont Blanc through our cabin-pod windows!"

"Right, I'll believe that when I see it. Wildestdreams eh? Come on, give us a nadger."

"Aren't we the lucky ones! Lucky you didn't chuck that ticket down the omniglopter."

Soon, they were on board the "Thetis" an old fashioned cruise liner, which had been renovated for this historic voyage. They steamed, though not literally, out of Scafell Pike harbour. There were thousands on board, but they had of course all paid huge amounts of money for their tickets. As lottery winners, Bax and Jayden were invited to sit on the captain's table and were served savoury Glob from silver tubes which descended from the ceiling, inserting a small feeding mouthpiece directly into their mouths. None of your re-constituted jelly fish either. Fishy, yes, despite the mass fish extinction of the early 40s, but with a tantalising aftertaste of seaweed. - a rare treat nowadays, given the circumstances around the seashores.

The captain, Blandon Coles, was friendly and affable. "If you think that was special, then try this. Bonsuck!". He pressed a fingerpod on the table and a different tube descended into their mouths.

"Mmmmh! Fabloid!" said Bax. "Sort of almost fruity deep compost with a hint of methane! – Boris! You're spoiling us!"

"Only for one night, mind," laughed Captain Coles. "A special treat on us!"

After dinner, Bax and Jayden held hands in the Totalitorium, along with a thousand other passengers, to admire the sea. The on-board host, Ray 'I kid you not' Sunshine, gave them a commentary, interspersed with jokes, and snatches of song. In his virtualised show, he talked and sang them through the dark oceans that surrounded them on all sides, taking them, virtually, deep beneath the waves to show then what was left of Amsterdam, and the Ile de France. Paris had been submerged in the 30s, as the oceans rose. He took them into a virtual Louvre, where the Monalisa gazed out at them through a glass darkly, and smiled with a sub-aqueous smile. The public now paid a lot of money to be fizzed around in submarbots to see the great treasures and icons of former ages.

"Fabloid!" murmured Jayden. "This holiday has everything - adventure, great cuisine and culture too!"

"Not too much culture I hope." remarked Bax. "Culture can spoil relaxation. Remember our President's motto: "Too much culture, too much joy, makes Jack a dull boy!"

"Yeah, let's keep things bland for the big highlight, tomorrow. No snogathons tonight then. Goodnight!" She kissed him insipidly on the cheek.

But the night was all too exciting. A double tornado passed close to the ship, throwing the ship violently up and down in the chaos of heaving waves. All round the ship, Glob and Glog was retched and vomited back up, only to be sluiced and swilled down different tubes, re-cycled and re-constituted into the next luxury on-board dinner, and eventually out into the seas above Geneva.

By morning, the seas were calm once more round the Alpine Fjords. The surround plasma-screens in the cabinbots woke the sleeping passengers to urge them to look out on the glorious island peak of Mont Blanc, or better still, come up to have the full surround 4D view.

Jayden and Bax held hands as they felt the Mont Blanc experience all around them, as they sat in the Totalitorium.

"I wonder," said Jayden, "if our grandchildren will be able to experience anything as grand as this in their lifetime?"

"No chance!" said Bax. "Mont Blanc is sinking 100 metres a year. They might just get a glimpse of the green mossy pointy bit at the top, if they hurry!"

"Holiday of a lifetime!" murmured Jayden, gazing at that grey tip, once so gleaming white. "At least of *OUR* lifetime! All gone by theirs!"

The Dinner Party from Hell - (Partying is Such Sweet Sorrow)

Tragically, I was assassinated by Putin, while I was an undercover reporter in Russia. Poisoned by a radio-active ice cream. But by a stroke of luck, my first assignment in the afterlife was as an undercover reporter at a covert gathering of erstwhile megalomaniacs, in a private dining room in the Inferno. My secret persona was Machiavelli, and my report was for the Tartarus Times.

Now, my medieval Italian was not perfect, but no matter – in the Underworld, everyone understands each other. I arrived at the elaborate portals of a stately dining room. I knocked, and the doors swung open. I was greeted by Alexander the Great, the convivial host of the feast of Persepolis. He showed me to the table. It was set for thirteen – one of them was for me. "Sit down Mr. ... er ...?".

"Just call me Machiavelli, or Mack," I said, shaking his hand.

There was a deafening rumble at the doors, and the second of the guests arrived, in a maelstrom of fire, mercury and whirling clouds. Huge and hairy, with beetling brows, a monster of a megalomaniac – it was Qin Shi Huangdi, the first emperor of China. He abruptly swept all the prepared hors d'oeuvres off the table, and sat down, with a huge pneumatic grunt.

"Charmed, I'm sure," said Alexander. "Mack, why don't you pour our guest a drink?"

I poured him a mercury on ice from a large jar, and it certainly stopped him grunting.

A chirpy ping-pong doorbell chimed, and in tumbled Hideyoshi, Domitian and Napoleon Bonaparte, all fighting to enter first. They sat down angrily and sulked.

"Oh, Genghis and Tamburlaine send apologies. They're on Fire Wheel duty just now," said Domitian, rubbing his hands spitefully.

"Oh, alright. Drinks everyone?" said Alexander. "Mack, be a darling and do the honours."

"Time to *flatter* princes." I murmured to myself. "The usual, gentlemen? Apocalypse cocktails all round?" I poured them each a glass of foaming putrescence.

"Delighted to meet you at last, Hideyoshi." I whispered, as I filled his glass. "You're my second favourite megalomaniac! It's the name, I think."

"Amazing feats of terror!" I murmured to Domitian, "Do draw up a coffin to make yourself more comfortable." (I had noticed several lined up on the far wall)

"Excellent conquest of Egypt, and ... er ... Europe ... almost, Sir" I purred to Bonaparte. He blushed.

"Just a quick obelisk takeaway, before conquering all of Europe, but that's another story," he replied.

Just then, Hitler and Stalin arrived, with explosive power, through the ceiling, and landed wrestling on the table.

"Gentlemen, let's be gentlemen!" exclaimed Alexander. "Let's try to have a civilized symposium, please, though there are still some missing. The seating arrangements must be strictly observed."

"Are there to be no ladies present?" repined Hideyoshi, known for his concubines.

"Ladies are not concerned with conquest," said Emperor Qin, with a sexist sneer, "except in my bed!"

At this they all laughed uproariously, making obscene gestures.

Just then, Mithridates himself emerged like a hologram, at the opposite end of the table, with a chest of phials, bottles, pots, obviously containing ... *substances*. He rose up, disarmingly charming.

"Apologies for my late 'beaming up', as they say. I had a few 'presents' to sort out for the occasion."

He was my third favourite megalomaniac, so I was extremely excited, and wanted to ask for an autograph – in all twenty-six languages he was fluent in.

There were some heated exchanges I will gloss over now, all recorded on my secreted recording device, about who should be seated at the head of the table. Domitian moved a coffin behind the spare seat, as though he was moving a chess piece. Silence fell, as the first course was served, though there was a lot of noisy gulching of dark matter.

Alexander, genial as ever, rose to speak, with a goblet smoking ominously.

"To all of us extreme powerbrokers, and the wonderful energy we brought to the otherwise static and rather dull world. We are technically dead, but our spirits, our souls, live on!"

There was foot-stamping and united cheers at this.

"Tell us the plan! Get on with it, you Greek Git!" shouted Hitler, with more than a veiled hint of racism.

"My plan," said Alexander, with a charismatic smile, "is simply this: with our immense powers, we could unite to conquer the world!"

There were cries of "But we're dead!" or "Not that old chestnut!" or "I'm not uniting with him!"

Hideyoshi and Emperor Qin rose with ceremonial swords and swiped violently. Luckily, no heads rolled.

"Not the living world, obviously ... I mean let's conquer the Afterlife, the World of the Dead."

Silence fell. No one had ever suggested such a thing before. It was known that the Afterlife was ruled by a sinister consortium, or gang of deities, such as Ahriman, Marduk, Lucifer, and a few extremely animistic – half-animal gangster gods from the likes of South America, Tibet and Australia. Hell, as we conceive it, is in fact just a province of the "Underworld", which is vaster than any country on Earth, being five-dimensional. It stretches both back in time, and forward. The Inferno, where they now sat, is just a tiny provincial parish within the vastness of Eternity. This was a bold idea and must be kept very hush-hush. There were extremely nasty punishments for insurrection, and these punishments lasted forever.

"Where is Saint Vladimir the Terrible, when you need him?" asked Napoleon.

"Oh, he became a Christian, so he doesn't count!" said Stalin.

"But he was 'sainted' for persecuting everyone else, a bit like us!" Hitler pointed out. "Being a Christian never stopped anyone being a despot."

Napoleon spoke out: "Aren't you being a trifle naïve, Alexander, to think we could ever agree, let alone decide the leader of this coup d'état? I would of course be the natural choice for General in any battle."

Disagreements broke out over this and blows and slicing swords were exchanged violently. This time, heads did roll, but were swiftly attached again. Mithridates was quietly mixing new cocktails. I helped him serve them out while the fracas went on.

"Surely poison won't work on the dead?" I whispered to Mithridates.

"Just a little experiment I've been working on, to kill not just the body, but the soul itself," he murmured.

The table was by now overturned, and the hellish feast lay scattered across the floor. The coffins were broken up. Mithridates announced:

"Machiavelli will serve cocktails, so we can re-establish the conviviality of villains. To Megalomaniacs everywhere!"

They rose as one, united briefly. Some of them quaffed the Mithridatic cocktail down, and after a brief pause, exploded loudly, in a plume of blue slime. This just left Alexander, Hideyoshi, and Qin at the table. I had to turn off my recorder quickly, because of feed-back.

Mithridates was writing notes.

"All part of my plan to eliminate competition. We are left with three remarkable generals, and a remarkable super-brain, to direct operations." He examined his long nails appreciatively.

"You didn't actually succeed with the Romans!" Alexander pointed out spitefully. "Not such a clever clogs, then!"

"The Romans cheated! It was not my fault. Anyway, you died too young to consolidate your vast conquest, remember, Alexander!"

"I conquered everywhere and unified Japan!" remarked Hideyoshi.

"I conquered everywhere, and united China, which is bigger!" said Qin.

"Gentlemen, please! Unity is needed, not bragging and blagging," said Alexander. "Machiavelli, we need a political advisor. You were good at that stuff. You wrote a textbook, didn't you?"

So it was, that I found myself, in under-cover disguise, as Machiavelli, actually having to give a bunch of megalomaniacs political advice – or else my cover would be blown.

"Oh, I never believed all that stuff, of course," I blurted. "I just told them what they wanted to hear. History has taught us all conquests are temporary, and all great leaders are mortal – a fever, a bonk on the head, an arrow through an eye ... and you're history ... forever!"

"But we are dead," said Qin, "and now that we're immortal, it's time we were in control of this vast unconquered empire of the immortals and become emperors for all Eternity! Now my tactic was a good one: I burned books, I buried 430 scholars alive, I built canals, and made 8,000 terracotta warriors to guard over me."

"Exactly," said Mithridates. "You lacked the brains behind the brawn. Now I have developed, through my scholarship of poisons, a weapon of mass destruction ... of SOULS!"

They all gasped. But suddenly, he turned on me, poison chalice in hand:

"Let's try it out. Machiavelli, you're not yourself today, are you? ... or rather, WHO are you? A spy? I always hated spies."

I'm pretending to be taking notes on my phone. Whose side was I on anyway? The Tartarus Times is perhaps just the voice piece of the powerbrokers, the sinister gangster-like controllers of the vast five-dimensional lands of the Dead. I am writing a text saying 'Help! HELP!!'.

Mithridates is approaching me with the Holocaust Cocktail. The other three are wrenching my head back and forcing the elixir of the ultimate death of the soul, down my throat! I am pressing 'Send' so you will know all this ...

Dead tone ... Dead Silence.

Emerging Truth

Certain signs, faint at first, had been gradually emerging. Hannah couldn't put her finger on it, but she felt a vague loss of control, as if others – or 'another', were making decisions for her.

There were the lovers, for a start. One after another, and all resulting is disastrous relationships. Would she ever have gone for Anthony … such an alpha male and always on some Rugby pitch? Or Julian, polar opposite, a poetic recluse who turned out to have sexual issues due to an unhappy abused childhood? Or even Ryan, loveable rogue and womaniser and ladies' man? They came and went thick and fast. But was it her doing? Did she even like any of them?

Then there were the 'Long-Losts': second cousins, usually unknown, some homeless, some political refugees from God-knows-where, turning up on her doorstep. And a long-lost school friend she couldn't even remember, recovering from anorexia, and staying six months before disappearing like a willow-the-wisp … literally. Did she have limitless extra spare rooms in her house for these long-term lodgers, exiles, and political refugees?

Who decided she would suddenly change careers from a hygienist to become a life coach and counsellor? Was it really herself, or some higher voice or 'finger in the sky' directing her every move? She felt that she herself needed counselling now. There was no follow-up. What happened to these people who came for soul-searching consultations on anything from suicide to divorce, neighbourhood grouches to road rage? And how had she ever qualified, or chosen this path? Surely, she would have needed a Ph.D. in Psychology at least? She felt so … out of her depth, beyond her comfort zone somehow. And who was this sinister Gerald, with his insinuating personality disorder, and bullying 'gaslighting' techniques?

Now things were coming to a head. She needed to know. Was she going out of her mind, out of herself, into uncontrolled mental space? Was she being controlled by some unseen berserk algorithm, of unknown origin? She would google it. There must be answers.

She started by googling her own name. Hannah Athene Silvester – Who is she? The answers were immediate and multiple. The first one was an entry updated on Wikipedia. Hannah Athene Silvester is a character in 'Lucifer Road', a popular award-winning soap opera about life on an ordinary estate in Worcestershire. Hannah has been an ongoing part of the series since childhood and is known best for her many disastrous love entanglements and work/life crises, in which the writers can discuss openly current issues and difficult topics with its growing audience of 65 million. It has been emerging in her most recent storyline, that Hannah has been suffering from an identity melt-down after a strange client called Gerald arrived for counselling and is inveigling her sanity with his own coercive controlling dystopian personality – a popular topical personality disorder.

Just below it said: If you have been affected by any of these issues, please contact:

www.BBC.co.uk/mentalemergencies/identitycrises

So now she knew. She wasn't even a real person at all. Just a fictional character in the nation's favourite soap opera. The pain and confusion of this was too much to bear alone. She typed in 'BBC forward-slash mental emergencies forward-slash identity crises.co.uk. and clicked. She must get help at once!

Surely the BBC, of all people, would know how to help …?

The Nobel Prize for Scientific Creativity

(Introduced by Professor Manuel Gregorovitz)

"Welcome, Ladies and Gentlemen, to the 2235 Nobel Science Award Winning History of Science lecture. I hope you all enjoyed the pre-lecture cocktails and nibbles and can now relax and enjoy some edifying morsels of scientific history!

It was way back in 2085, that a small group of Scottish researchers, led by Dr Jean O'Farrell, won the Nobel Science Award for a remarkable invention. No one could possibly have predicted its far-reaching impact. But, nevertheless, it was hailed as a breakthrough in the evolution of Mankind, no less.

The prize-winning invention was DNA-based eradication of all evil genes in men and women. The 'Emulsionator'. Any tendencies however big or small, towards evildoing, anger, jealousy, malice, or megalomania, could be 'emulsionated' out of babies in utero. Women were then routinely 'emulsionated' during pregnancy. There was a worldwide hope that a generation completely devoid of any leanings towards evil, would change the world everlastingly for the better.

By 2095, a group of Chinese scientists, led by Professor Juno Ching, developed the handheld Emulsionator which could be applied to any adult, so that the older generation could also be inoculated against any selfish or self-seeking behaviours. The implications for Peace on Earth and future happiness had never been rosier. People happily settled down to a life of pure altruism, and together, united, they defeated the world problems of global warming, giving up all individual selfish desires for the common good of all societies across the planet. People went to extraordinary lengths to facilitate their neighbours' comfort, safety, and security. There was no theft. No scams or tricks, no murders, or genocides. Everyone put all their intelligence and strength into solving the big problems of pollution, population explosion and politics. If there was any slight conflict it was about who could do the most to serve their communities. It was heaven on Earth, as you can imagine my friends ... or NEARLY!

Except for one thing. A small group of North Korean scientists led by Dr. Kim Yong Kom, had somehow eluded the Emulsionating process and had holed up in a bunker north of Pyongyang in 2137. Like all good scientists, they had set themselves a challenge: to produce one perfect embryo which had all the good genes and altruistic tendencies, totally erased. A child that was completely 100% EVIL! This child, the now all too famous Kim Kong King, was reared in complete secrecy, attacking, or killing all who came near him. Eventually, as an unmanageable teenager with vast and horrible ambitions, he was let loose on the world. A tyrant had been nurtured – a creature of infinite evil without any boundaries of inhumanity. An incubus of pure malice without a wisp of compassion or empathy in his DNA, let loose on a population of kind, altruistic human beings, with no inkling of what was about to be unleashed. They literally just rolled over and submitted to conquest without a fight.

And now, my dear audience, we who study history in 2217, know how frightful the outcome of a scientific experiment can be. We are descended from the results of his disastrous breeding programme. Scientists, so full of ideas, cannot predict how their Nobel Prize-winning inventions might be manipulated – as we great-great-grandchildren of the few survivors well know!

So now I must reveal to you that I am not the well-meaning erudite Professor Manuel Gregorovitz, Guardian of Historical and Scientific knowledge, that you thought I was. No, my friends, I have tricked you. I am King Kong Klan, and my DNA 'Evil' count is 98%, the direct inheritor of King Kong King the Mighty. History teaches us many lessons. It should teach us all the pitfalls and repetitions. I have faked this revival of the Nobel Prize for Science in order to award myself for … re-imagining the 'Emulsionator' as the 'Re-Evilator!'

Now I must warn you that I have randomly spiked all your drinks and nibbles with a toxic radiation poison. Some of you therefore will randomly die, horribly, in the next few minutes, and others will be herded into secret bunkers to breed new mutations devoid of any altruistic genes. I am the living embodiment and apotheosis of our single male ancestor Kim Kong King. I will rule the world with my Re-Evilator. History repeats itself and re-evilates.

Some of you are beginning to turn green and are sickening. I may be 98% evil, but I am 2% squeamish. I must go. Goodbye, my friends. The Nobel Prize for Science is mine … ALL MINE!

On the Brink

The cloaked figure stood silhouetted on the bridge, at the edge of the parapet, looking down at the waters beneath.

"Oh my god," she thought. "He's going to leap into the churning waters and end it all!"

She ran forward and stood below him, arms resting on the bridge.

"No!" she yelled. "Don't do it! I beg you to think again! Your life is unique and precious. Your family will be heartbroken … your lover distraught!

He didn't answer, just stood, contemplating the waters below as if pausing for flight.

"We all go through crises." She thought of her own, and how she too had been tempted to end it all. But she'd come through it, changed jobs, met solid Gerald, got a home with him, and settled more or less, give or take a few pills here and there, to keep her steady. She'd just had a few and felt suddenly strong.

"Have you tried medication?" she asked hopefully. No answer still. "Alcohol? Heaven forbid … it's a depressant. Drugs maybe? Do you need rehab?" Still a strong silence.

"Maybe you need to phone a friend? … Oh, I don't mean like in the millionaire quiz, just someone to stand by you, to hold your hand?" No answer.

"I will be your friend. Give me your hand to hold. Just please, come down. Please! Change your mind. Suicide is so … final, so drastic!"

The river below swirled and boiled beneath them, so menacingly. What a dreadful end it would be.

"You must come down to me now!"

Suddenly an ambulance flashed past casting blue lights across the bridge, and the figure on it. As she turned, she looked up at him, and realised, in a flash, that this was no suicidal man about to leap, but a statue, a bronze statue, marking the centre of the bridge.

"Sorry! ..." she faltered. "I thought you were ..." But the statue stared stonily above her, surveying the wide rushing river.

"You...You ... effffff##ing IMPOSTER!" she yelled, and she seized a heavy metal traffic sign about 'Temporary Bridge Alterations' and thwacked the statue across its bronze ankles. Then with a gargantuan mighty push, she dislodged it from its plinth. It teetered on its legs, tottered sideways, rocked forwards, and fell from the bridge into the foaming waters.

"How DARE you! You total BASTARD!"

Then she saw the writing on the plinth. 'To St Christopher, guardian of all who travel over dangerous waters'.

"Oh God!" She leant over the edge of the bridge in time to see the statue sink beneath the dark waves and disappear in a sudden act of surprise suicide …

Or perhaps 'Statue-tory Execution?' ...

Random Acts

He had always been obsessed with 'The Dice Man', the book where a man made every decision according to the throw of a dice. The Gamble, thrill of the throw. The utter commitment too, to see the riddle through. He'd taken risks on the throw of the dice and won. Now, as he sat in his penthouse suite, he wanted one last throw. He lined up his options:

[6] Give a million quid to an unknown vagrant.

[5] Perform a random act of kindness to anyone in any way.

[4] Become a vagrant for a week and sleep rough.

[3] Commit a random act of violence, and risk arrest.

[2] Commit murder quietly and undetectably.

[1] Do nothing and have a drink.

Even as he wrote this last, he found himself already disappointed. He wanted a thrill – one last adrenaline rush. He didn't actually want to murder anyone, of course not. But if he threw a 2, he knew he would have to, compelled by this omniscient 'Dice Man' in his head.

He took the dice in two hands, shook it and threw. It came to rest at 5, a random act of kindness. Easy one! A bit of money, chocolates maybe, a bottle of whiskey perhaps. He would dress as a homeless person and surprise a fellow sufferer. Easy ...

Outside it was snowing. He had an old mack, torn down one side, a woolly hat, and old wellies. He put a belt round his mack, put a roll of notes, a bottle of whiskey, some biscuits and the dice, into an old Tesco bag. Then smiled at his reflection of his new self in the gold Rococo mirror in the hall. Perfect! He would soon get this easiest of options over and done.

He wandered alone under Waterloo Bridge where he knew he would find the homeless, the dispossessed. Though in darkness he looked for a person who most deserved his kindness.

"Oy! This is our patch Skunky!" Dark hooded figures leapt on him. He saw the flash of their knives in the gloom. "Grab 'is bag!" called one who hung back in the shadows. "'Oo does he think 'e is! Slit 'is froat so 'e won't squeal!"

They leapt on him, randomly ripping his clothes with Stanley knives, punching, and kicking him, even pissing on him as he lay in a gutter.

"Stop there!" called a soft but urgent voice. "Leave him right now!" A small girl, no more than 15, sprang brave as a ringmaster into the circling predators.

"You're just a snivelling girly girl. Wotchit, kid … you're out of your depth!" they snarled.

But she stood over his body. "Leave him to me. He's mine now." She said quietly. Unbelievably, they skulked off, carrying his torn Tesco bag with the whiskey, the biscuits, the roll of money, and the dice.

She knelt beside him, examining him with a small torch. "You're in a bad way. I'm here to help. Here's my sleeping bag. I'll roll you onto it. I have water to wash your wounds and soothe your bruises. Then you must sleep … who are you? Why are you here?"

But all he could say, or groan, was "Kindness … **you** are the … random … act …" before he passed out. The girl looked after him for a whole week, and in all his life he had never met such bravery and such a random act of kindness and humanity.

Solitude - Virtually

It was that one mistake, right at the beginning, that had put them there, in the virtual chatroom. There was a group of them, setting up a weekly meeting on Zoom. None of them knew quite how it worked. It proved a learning curve that quickly turned into a never-ending spiral into nothing.

That was, what? One or two years ago ... maybe more? Mary didn't know. She only knew that peering at the tiny icons at the top of the webpage, she had tentatively pressed 'Invite a Friend', and typed in Tim's name. She was about to add the other four names when she noticed 'Add' and clicked on it. And BANG! That was it.

Suddenly at the bottom of the screen, her picture appeared, looking down at her own tablet. And there was Tim, displayed large across the main screen, looking surprised and unnerved at the sudden unexpected summons.

The strange sensation of being 'out of body' struck her then. She was not present in 3D body form, looking at the screen. She was inside the video itself, trapped and disembodied. But so too was Tim. They were marooned in a virtual chat room, but unable to press the 'Leave Meeting' button.

In the first year or two they had kept going, hoping that one of the other writers would press 'End Meeting', or that someone, a partner, or friend, or even a computer hacker, would unplug their computers and end it. They would suddenly bounce back into their real corporeal bodies and be able to live their 3D lives again. Be able to wash, change their clothes, eat, clean their teeth. Be free. But it just didn't happen.

They chatted, of course. Went through their lives, their past histories, their loves, their bugbears. They recited poetry, sang songs, and passed endless time. They shared secrets, frustrations, and fears. They shared helpless silence, tears, bereavement, arguments, and blighted hopes.

Then suddenly their virtual chatroom was invaded, but not by their long-lost writer friends. And not in a good way. There was a sudden eruption onto the central screen of Gary, a crazy shouting tattooed man, with a problem. He said he was a blogger. But they soon realised he was a **troll**. He had been invading chatrooms and video conferences, randomly, ranting about 'Taking Back Control!' and 'F**k the liberal elite!' And in between he was thoroughly objectionable and obnoxious to them personally. Mary was a '*f**king numbat*'. And Tim was a 'spazzy *bollock!*'

Somehow, he pushed himself into the main talking centre of the screen, while Mary and Tim were reduced to minute squeaking icons at the bottom. And he was an insomniac psychopath too, ... angry, shouting, violently kicking all night in his 2D video box. The audio sound went up to maximum. Unbearable! It was Jean-Paul Sartre's Hell alright, locked up together in Hell's own chatroom. They longed to return to the relative solitude of the two of them onscreen, in occasional civilised conversation, albeit it muted.

Gary threatened to summon his friends to the chatroom. But try as he might, kicking and shouting and swatting at every icon that came up, he couldn't find 'Add Friend'. But that only made him swear more abusively at them. Eventually, he broke down in tears and sobbed his heart out. He confessed about his abusive childhood, his violent father, his paedophile uncle, his uncaring care home. They listened and were kind. He told them tearfully, that they were his only real friends. That he had 'accidentally' killed his best mate ... "'E ran into my fist!". He'd abused his wife and relentlessly bullied his kids. They'd all left for a refuge. The only thing that made him happy was **TROLLING**, and how was it possible to have ended up stuck with 'two f**king FAIRIES?!!!' So, then he started yelling foul abuse at them all over again.

It was impossible for Tim and Mary to ever have a reasonable conversation. Their virtual selves could only operate in the tiny virtual space of the icon. If only they could reach out and press 'Audio Off!' But it was Gary 24/7... on Max.

Then, after what? ... (3 years? Maybe 5?), Gary was suddenly summoned to another meeting: The NFB, or National Fascist Brigade, and he suddenly etherised, leaving no trace of himself. It was Mary and Tim, back to the joint disembodied solitude of their virtual lives online. But only for a while, because Gary, unfortunately, supported by his Tech-savvy Neo Nazi friends, decided to summon Tim, with 'Add Friend', to their own Gotterdammerung gathering, celebrating Hitler's death ... where poor Tim would be virtually kicked and mocked forever for being a 'Philosophy Ph**ker'. (Sorry Tim, that is part of the story!)

Mary was left, alone, in her solitary chatroom, of her own foolish making. In disembodied isolated *SOLITUDE* ... Forever and ever. (Sorry Mary. That's in the story too).

Writers Block … by the Monster itself.

This one looked like a synch, sitting blankly with a pen dandling uselessly between fingers like a damp cigarette.

I approached, cracking my knuckles, figuratively, so to speak. Easy prey. Half a page written already. I looked over her shoulder. Oh my God! Not another blooming Landscape poem! Who do these wannabe writers think they are? Who wants to read dull stuff about Yorkshire walls and bare brown flippin' hills? Porn. Thrills. Gruesome murders. That's what sells.

The other writers were scribbling away, predictably heading into deadeningly heightened prose, or unedited ramblings of no consequence whatsoever.

"I'll take this one from the inside!" I told myself, rubbing my invisible hands with relish. "A pushover!" I thought as I entered her brain through one ear. I soon found myself struggling in the inner swamp of her internal negativity. I tuned in, curious, to hear the neurological rag-and-bone shop of her inner dialogue.

"You'd be better off writing a shopping list for Friday!" Right Brain opined sensibly.

"Oh come on, you've only got a few minutes to get this written…get it finished!" Left Brain urged.

"Try to remember that idea you had. The landscape and memory, sort of thing, this morning." Ego chipped in enthusiastically.

"All the others are so much more articulate," Inferiority Complex countermanded.

"You've got it in you to write a bestseller!" Id doing its usual burst of grandiose thinking. And so on and so on. I could see that I wasn't going to get a word in edgeways … ME! Writers Block Monster, from my Loch Ness of the subliminal subconscious! – The great Wielder of the Giant Red Pen…and when I say red pen, I really mean RED Scythe, like Medieval Death … only to Writers.

But there was so much noise going on in this writer's head! Such harassment, legalise, and internal self-abuse, that even I was side-lined.

The subject seemed to be responding. The paper lay empty like a white desert of pain, the pen had slipped. Just one sad doodle in the corner.

"CAN'T! SHOULDN'T! MUSTN'T!" yelled the inner phantoms. They were doing me out of a job!

"Silence!" I shouted in an over-blocking boom. "I require a moment of silence to advise my client.!" They all started shouting back that she was their client. Who did I think I was?

"You know me. I am the Dreaded Writers' Block Monster. The ultimate LAST word, literally! This wannabe writer doesn't even need your elementary snarking and ridiculing of

her pathetic poetry and lamentable prose. She needs ..." (I amazed myself). She needs more complex thought- counselling. Otherwise, NONE of us will have any fun at her expense. I mean, what's interesting about destroying the hopes of an utter dead loss? We should build her up first, inflate her ego, and then utterly knock her flat. Then finish her off with a finale of master-blocking!"

They all fell silent. the Left Brain, the Right Brain, the Ego, the Id, and all the other minor inferiorities and self-harming complexes, all turned down their volume.

Then I surprise myself again. "Tell the Negative Committee that sits inside your head to FUCK off!" I whispered in her ear.

And my god ... she listened, and with a resounding "FUCK off!" she lifted her pen and wrote and wrote and wrote.

Such a really good and interesting novel it became. Widely read across the world in fact. And then she wrote another, and a book of poetry. She found her voice, her own genuine voice, not the inner voices, but her own true voice.

"She's overcome her inner demons!" said her fellow writers. They were right!

Me? Defeated? Well, a bit I suppose. But she's on her third novel now, and I'm hooked. I want to find out what happens in the end. So, I'm going to step back for now ... And do some reading.

Printed in Great Britain
by Amazon